I0839293

PING-PONG (RALLY'S ON)

RELATING TO PRIDE OF SELF & OUR POLITICAL MIASMA

By Joseph K. Goldstein

By the same author

The America Series:

Things of Concern- a Dissertation relating to the State of the World and the State of Mind

All Things Relate- a View of the U.S. Economy

Land of Opportunity- Opportunities and Guarantees in America

Ping-Pong (Rally's On)- Relating to Pride of Self & Our Political Miasma

The Evolver Series:

Two Visions- Pathways in Nature Artwork- (with Donna Jean Goldstein)

Look at Me- My Journey through Time and Experience-(a rather private diary)

Moments of Impact- My Personal Inquiry Relating to the Formation of Self

Conversatility- Conversations: Meanings within an Exchange

ISBN -13: 978-1985585584

ISBN -10: 1985585588

Goldstein, Joseph K. 1938-
Ping-Pong (Rally's On)/ Joseph K. Goldstein- 1st Ed.   P.cm.

    1. Politics- 21st Century-commentary
    2. Sociology- 21st Century- commentary
    3. Psychology- 21st Century-commentary
    4. Self-Help-21st Century-commentary

CreateSpace
North Charleston, SC

DEDICATION AND ACKNOWLEDGEMENTS

You know what, this book is really a result of the current mind-set within this country. It isn't easy to live on pins and needles, but politics has become a major consideration today, and so there is lots of food for thought to churn around. So what this is about is that dedication can only be to the grand group called citizens of the United States of America, and how up-bringing and mind-set have placed such a dichotomy within us. Not to say that is wrong, because all sides have degrees of validity to support their feelings, thoughts, emotions, and thus the intellectual abyss becomes filled with the yin-yang of reality. "How about this, but on the other hand…", was once a byword, but now it is in your face "oh yeah, well let me tell you…". Exposure to that confrontational condition is what has provided impetus to write this book. I already had a certain amount of predisposition, as you would see if you looked at the books in my "America Series", but now that I see us so divided, I want to thank both sides of the equation for forcing my thought process beyond what it had been.

And so I dedicate and acknowledge that it is my friends, my neighbors, and my fellow citizens that have inspired me to place these thoughts on paper.

Joe Goldstein

PING-PONG (RALLY'S ON)
RELATING TO PRIDE OF SELF
& OUR POLITICAL MIASMA
A Series of Discussions Relating to Accomplishment of
Goals, Self-Worth, and the Current State of U.S. Affairs

Table of Contents

FOREWARD 11
ARTICLES ON THE PRIDE OF SELF 13
   ARTICLE 1   INTRODUCTION 14
   ARTICLE 2   ON THE SUBJECT OF "RIGHTS" 17
     Figure 1 New Brighton(China Beach)- Majesty 20
   ARTICLE 3   SELF-WORTH: AND TODAY'S CURRENT
STATE OF AFFAIRS 21
   ARTICLE 4   LOOKING TO THE LIGHT AND LESSONS TO
BE LEARNED 27
     Figure 2 New Brighton- Simplicity 38
   ARTICLE 5   MORE ON HEALTH CARE AND
GOVERNMENT 39
   ARTICLE 6   HUMANITARIANISM 42
   ARTICLE 7   ON TERRORISM-A SCARY REVERSAL 45
   ARTICLE 8   I AM TOO, PROUD OF MYSELF 47
     Figure 3 Twin Lakes- Profusion 49
   ARTICLE 9   SURPRISES 50
   ARTICLE 10   BUDGETS, DEFICITS, AND IOU'S 53
   ARTICLE 11   TERRORIST MIND-SET 55
   ARTICLE 12 IMMIGRATION 58
     Figure 4 Kokola, Kaua'i- Gateway 62
   ARTICLE 13 SEX & POWER 63
CONCLUSIONS: SO WHERE ARE WE GOING? 67
ADDENDUM 1 PROGRAM STUDY: HEALTH CARE 69
REFERENCES 89

FOREWARD

When I originally conceived a theme for this book, my mind had then-president Barack Obama and his administration's proclivities as a fore-thought and I wanted to deal solely with their approach to individualism. Now I have Donald J. Trump looming in the spotlight as well, and so I decided on this "ping-pong" title, because we have been doing just that- instead of developing a clear and effective strategy for the future of our country, we have two political parties, each in turn, trying to force their ideologies and propensities on us all. No regard for ALL OF US, only for their own political goals. Looky-Lou, at two sides of a very sad tale. At first I thought of both candidate's respective rises in our political system as interesting , although now-president Trump doesn't even get to be in the crowd except by (amazingly enough) election, and Barack only as an ideological neophyte at his time of election. So what happened to our political system that we have come to this state? I think it is the free enterprise system and our partial democracy that has allowed these two to surface from their origins and break out into the grown-up world, little prepared as they each were. Each looked down from their respective ivory towers, Obama from an intellectual setting offering that each of us is truly our brother's keeper in that what someone wants, they should have because they deserve it. And the Donald from an environment of massive bullying, where bucks and position speak louder than words. Is it blasphemous to so state these two anomalies? I always thought that if nothing else, the political system went hand in hand with diplomacy, and that the ultimate goal of this system in the United States was the welfare of our nation. Not a nation of welfare, and not an isolationist gamble.
So here I am, putting together a forward that tries to retain the essence of my original conception, but recognizing the amazingness of surprise. It is interesting now to be looking at two administrations and their practices, and recognizing that the next administration will probably follow in the footsteps of one of these. So although the names will change, will the tactics? Will the agendas? Oh my, what are we going to get stuck with, or can our two inept major parties truly come up with fresh ideas and fresh faces. I do not

believe the Democrats will change their agendas, but I do believe that the Republicans had better get a grip on their ideology.

You know, I have finally come to appreciate the term "sick and tired". I am that. Sick and tired of experiencing this ping-pong game of political ideologies. Sick and tired of having my intellect and emotions forcibly enmeshed in this mess. Sick and tired of seeing the threats to my financial status. Sick and tired of the constant threat of war somewhere. Sick and tired of thinking "cheer up, things could be worse", and when I cheer up, sure enough, things get worse. Politics is an intellectual abyss, filled with dogma, rationalization, self-interest- the pushing of an agenda. Diplomacy does not seem to be a part of the process. Diplomacy is the art of working together and accomplishing; especially something that satisfies all. And I would like to see it applied nation-wide and world-wide. Well, perhaps this will be my significant attempt to glean lessons from this process, although frankly, I think many more exciting lessons may be forthcoming. (Perish the thought!!!)
With this book, started as a commentary on life and on the 2008 and 2012 administrations, has evolved a comparison of the political realities in America today. I bear in mind that "prior results do not guarantee future outcome", so hope is not only still adrift but also alive. Remember "I can't take it anymore"? Tha's me now, and that's because the process has completely let every citizen down, and has taken aim at our institutions with the intent of marginalizing them from confidence in self to confidence in bail-out and dole. Darn it. And even worse, we have mob-mentality in the political process- "follow me blindly and I will lead you down the path to righteousness". And don't kid yourself, they are trying.

As an aside, I have added some sketches made over the past years, they are really about what this country offers-goodness, simplicity, nature. The reason they are here is that they remind me that the ping-pong game is a piece of life's yin-yang, and these sketches balance my diatribes about our political system.

ARTICLES ON THE PRIDE OF SELF
(This is only partially about Prides of Lions)
A Series of Discussions Relating to Accomplishment

ARTICLE 1   INTRODUCTION

At some time in my early teens I came to realize that what I was could be translated into what I wanted, and wanted to be. It was going to be what I had mastery of through my own capabilities that would lend of themselves to me being able to obtain what I wanted out of life; that I would be the one that had to produce to so obtain. Here is an exchange of energy, a sense of barter really, trading my outputs for my desires, and making some sort of social and financial contract that would result in mutual benefit to the parties concerned (one of whom is me, by the way). That is what money is used for- simply an arbitrary measure of worth, no intrinsic value, but valued through agreement as to what worth it is assigned against a product. Not the other way around, because basics are that we can easily do without money, it's just a convenience; but there would certainly be a burden to once-again having to lug a cart of wood over to your local butcher to get a side a beef.
The essence of it all is self-worth, your own ability to produce what is tradable to fulfill your own desires, needs, and requirements. This segued into further appreciation of capitalism and the worth of man and his outputs[1]. And further, after a significant lecture series, came an added dimension of regard for property, both physical and intellectual[2].

Well, what this whole thing is about relates to attitude. The 2008 and 2012 Presidential Elections have still essentially freaked me out, because looking at issues rather than personalities, these were elections focusing on socialism vs. individuality. Never was it so clear as when now-two-time-President Obama stated that his was a policy of income redistribution and that's what taxes were all about. And here I thought they were strictly for running the essentials of government. I wonder what happened to the concept that what is yours is yours- to spend, to give, to hoard, to save, to invest, to squander. AARGHHH, I fear the backslide. It is too easy to say "gimme", not quite so easy to put things together and do for yourself, I guess.

And of course, the 2016 election offered that in a free market economy everyone would be given the opportunity to move forward, including the opportunity to explore the many paths to obtaining the best results for oneself.   The uphill struggles that some of these paths require are just part of life.   So it bothers me to see that it is the easy way out that is still being proffered by a large part of our currently elected government and verified by a large percentage of the populace.   It gets back to what "Government" is for, and what it is all about. I believe it is formed strictly to PROTECT the RIGHTS of its citizenry.   Get into the definitions and see about protect and about rights.

And the 2016 elections offered a fascinating view of discontent. We elected a man whose background offered to reorient our perspective into one of pride of self, of focus on the original tenets of our government. Of course that would be a wild swing from a socialistic goal to one of full support of free enterprise. Problems were certainly to be expected, based not only on background, but on the method of the campaign-innuendos, insults, lack of specifics, potential withdrawal from making world affairs a main goal- all portends of possible concern. But the Clinton machine self-destructed and the Trumpster became the final choice. But sadly, the projection of him becoming "presidential" in mind and thought has not yet transitioned into reality. His methods remain those learned in the business environment- bluster and bluff, then negotiate to what you really want. When in business, money and power talk louder than words, and so it is easier to bull your way forward with a minimum of diplomacy, and a maximum of bluster. However, each bluster brings opposition, each bluff brings vitriolic response.

Well that dichotomy between mind-sets is what this missive is all about, and so let's move on into deep but somewhat previously charted waters.

The "Journals of Ayn Rand"[3] offers some major insights. She was an avid proponent of individualism and the recognition that the essence of man (as he exists on this planet) is his ego. All her work wrapped around and emanated from this concept, but what I see is that the things that are happening today are exactly the reverse. Since the Democratic Party under the guidance of Barack Obama had taken the reins of government, Rand's antithetical concept of second-handedness had really come to the fore- the cult of "give me, I deserve, I have the right to," are part of the very things that "The Fountainhead" and "Atlas Shrugged" used as anti-themes. And so I developed a really directed notion of what upset me, of what bothered me, of what I saw happening around me, in so many parts of the world.

Rand noted that if individual man helped society rise, then typically collectivism reared its ugly head to bring down the society, usually within 150 years or so. If this observation is correct, that puts the USA on a collision course with disaster, because the affluence afforded by individualism and personal control is being challenged by the second-hand takers. They are the ones who look around and say that they are trying to do "good" for others, when in reality they are leveling things and doing poorly for most.

And diametrically opposed is the Trump Doctrine. His "America First" has a good ring to it, because it implies looking out for our own good, and *then* to see how it also helps others. Well, that goes along with some of my basic beliefs about Property. The working definition of property is- everything about a person- beliefs, credos, word, ideas, physical belongings- it is a cult of selfishness. But wait, that is not the totality of the concept, because as each of us *respects* the property of others, then the word respect takes on new meaning. Now it would mean that no one takes from someone else without their permission, thus the concept of mutuality, of giving freely and taking with concurrence. Well, that could be what the Trump Doctrine is attempting, but the man has a specific personality developed over his many years and his many dealings, and he brings it with him into the office of Commander-In-Chief and President of These United States. No diplomacy, no suavity, simply bull-in-your-face. Is this the persona of choice for a leader of the free world? Well, that's to be seen. An awful lot of people disagree, although some of that angst is based more on Hillary and the Democratic Party losing than Trump winning.

THE REST OF THE RIDE STARTS HERE

ARTICLE 2   ON THE SUBJECT OF "RIGHTS"

Not talking about right vs. left, not talking about conservative right vs. liberal left, but about those things that are either inalienable, God-given, a ukase, or obtained by due-process. They are each in separate categories with respect to origin and compartmentalization. Definitions first:

- <u>protect</u>- "to shield from injury, to guard".
- <u>right</u>-   "something to which one has just or lawful claim."

OK, let's just remember those words for the time being.

Civilization came about because people found that it was advantageous to socially and economically combine rather than to be totally separate. Trade-offs occurred, where-in convenience easily won out against the extreme of living separately and totally fending for oneself (that meant food, clothing, shelter, protection). As well, there is an ingrained social need for the company of others like oneself. This is pretty simplistic, but it is an attempt to sum up the essence of the source of living within a community. It could have been pretty easy, because physical strength was the least common denominator in earlier times. It got coupled with intelligence to sift up the leadership. Wow, talk about 100 words or less.

The trade-off expanded in terms of scope of requirements, because sophistication reared its pretty head, and complexity entered the equation.   This is where leadership became the result of a combination of requirements, and resulted in selection of what could be termed "the best way and the best person". I still have in mind walking around with the largest weapon, but now that becomes attenuated by how craftily you swing it.

So what am I trying to say? People got together in a societal mix to achieve a basic level of existence easier than when they were not in the mix. That gets into shared tasking and specialization, because as some things are no longer necessary for a person to do, then more time is available to do other things. Such division of labor seemed a natural, and people became better at what they were able to focus on. Affluence, the wonder of civilization, reared its beautiful head in the simplest of ways-more free time, more time to focus on other things. BUT HERE'S THE RUB.

Affluence is a byproduct of the diligence required to produce it, it's a boot-strapping process. Accumulating the wherewithal which results in affluence is typically a work-hard process. Sure, there are the inheritors of circumstance or wealth, but for all the rest of us, it takes something of ourselves to produce the result. Could be sweat, could be brain, could even be the exercise of a likable personality, but whatever, it comes from you. Very little is considered a "right", not even survival. Once a society is formed though, it develops its own set of established rules. This is the start of what a society is all about- the modus operandi of interactions, and the things (tangible and intangible) that the society offers.

The interaction portion begs the question "what is the purpose of the society?" The word government fits in here, because the society requires some interactive guidelines in order to operate effectively, and this is where purpose translates into being. In a utopian environment, all things would mesh naturally, but it takes a major educational effort to instill support for such a methodology as a well-founded civilization, and in the interim, something needs to be set in place well before the actions become natural.

Mankind currently has many different governing methods and societal mores in place, all of them the results of the way different societies evolved. Various operating models currently in practice include democracy, capitalism, socialism, dictatorship, laissez-faire, and you can fit the rest as sub-elements somewhere within these five categories. So we have the governing and the governed, and how they operate within the guidelines of these definitions.

A democracy, whether limited or total, offers citizens choice of detailed governance. Capitalism gears towards allowing the free market forces to work and sift out how a society runs. Socialism focuses on the specific needs of the people and uses the lowest common denominator to pull on all strata to satisfy that need. A dictatorship allows delegation of authority to lie within the control of a leader and his selected advisors. Laissez-faire is an attempt to let things simply bubble or bumble along,

Which of these works, and how well, depends on the history and mind-set of the governed. Each of these is found in some operating form today.

Figure 1 New Brighton(China Beach)- Majesty

ARTICLE 3   SELF-WORTH: AND TODAY'S CURRENT STATE OF AFFAIRS

Let me start by saying it is not my intent to initiate any immediate change in mind-set, nor obviously can I modify current events. Rather, it is my goal to start a thought-provoking process of recognition, then transition and growth, aimed at re-vitalizing the concepts of individualism and pride in self. This must begin with the examination of where we are today.

I am having a tough time with the state of things in the world right now- aren't you? This whole thing is no longer about the past, but about learning what went wrong *then*, correcting it *now*, and moving *ahead*. Managing transition is really the key. That means to approach the goal, you follow a path that will get there, and how well this path is mapped and managed is the challenge. This is where I am having trouble, because what I actually see in place over these last two political ideologies, is not really a path to a recovery, but a path being charted to put us in a direction that lowers what we are to be; with those promoting it acting within a riotous routing of destructive integration of "objectives of reaction". Such people are ideologically hard-wired , and by gosh, they'll get it done!!!! Utopian objectives are probably buried within their goals, but the groups are ignoring that which established this country's baseline, the engine that generated our ability to even be where we are now. And on the other hand, we now have a president who is applying his own personal rules of business, based upon "bullying negotiation", which means threats are fine, and "I hope I have not exceeded the threshold", because if so, then bankruptcy is the only out. In the case of a country, that means war or world-ostracism.

So, what is going on?   Firstly, I feel we are beginning to overlook some of the basic premises upon which this greatest country of ours was founded. Foremost, it feels like there was surely an attempt at reversal by the prior administration of the sacred institution of individualism; "that ability to convert our own feeling of self-worth into the products needed for forming, directing, and living our lives". This is not esoteric, but a statement about the basis of everyone's personal view of life, it is how each of us accumulates the tools of survival, and gives us the ability to attain our own level of affluence definition. These things I talk about are not just (my) ideals, they are the realities existing around us every moment, observable in every action and in every-thing that is near and dear to us, including those things that are ours, and those things that we use, as we move along in our lives.

And secondly, a reversal of past policy as instituted by this new administration, one that says "America First", a good goal, but it must be tempered with a recognition that we are one of the world's societies, that we represent something big, that we all had been on the way to world-wide open communication through trade agreements which would have shrunk the world to a communicative and manageable size.

Take a look- it's hard to doubt that there is a trend charting its way towards downfall.

In taking that look, let me offer a premise for use in your own critical analysis:

We should all operate within a common framework of morality; simply stated **"What is yours is yours, and what belongs to someone else is not yours."** That's it. (That, by the way, is the cornerstone of our societal pact, the building block that supports the reality of self-worth. It is the real golden rule paraphrased: "give unto others if you wish to give unto others"). It is the translation of private property from ideal to real world, and is a cornerstone for the trust we place when we join together to make civilizations. There is a definition implicit within this moral input, which is that your property (which means your life, your physical possessions, and your intellectual output) belongs to **you**. Give if you wish (definition of charity), but for goodness sake, do not just take, nor allow to be taken without your consent.

There we have it, the critical parameter. Now we can examine what could be called part of life's mission statement, commensurate with the ideals of the founding fathers, translated into objectives that are the pillars supporting this country. Then we can look at programs designed to maintain our perspective.

But first: the nature and purpose of government. Government is the representation of and by the citizen for the sole intent of protection of citizen rights to life, liberty, and the pursuit of happiness. "Do what you will so long as you don't affect others without their personal permission." Sound familiar? Those guys knew what they were talking about when they wrote the Declaration and the Constitution.

OK, having said all this, then what am I talking about, and where is its relevance to today?

It starts with one of our recent past's "cause-celebs": the mortgage situational melt-down, it translates into the bail-outs, and segues, for example, into the latest considerations for health-care and beyond. Common thread is government and intervention with the free market system.

The free market system has some premises of its own, starting with "what you sow is what you reap". There has been a consequence to the misguided idea that well-developed financial ground rules and safeguards involving lending principles could be easily modified and would then produce exactly what was expected. Henry Hazlitt[4], one of the great 20th century economists, pointed out that as soon as control of any one thing is implemented, the need for control spreads, and spreads, and spreads. When the bar was lowered by the government regarding safe/ marginal/toxic loans and redefined to allow "those people less financially-substantial" to obtain mortgages, it came as no surprise that the lending industry began a bob and weave to accommodate. After all, it was at government ukase. The "ARM" (adjustable rate mortgage) was a good idea whose time had come. And right along with it came the risk associated with an unknown future. The balance point between investment and gamble shifted. That idea of balance wasn't anything new, but shame on those involved who had not done the research to quantify their risk. (Or, maybe they had, and had accepted that risk.) Everyone looked and projected an eventual rosy future. For those borrowing it looked like going out on a limb was a fine gamble. Note the word gamble, not investment. For the lender, the basic premise was business, that a company is formed to make a profit (albeit with secondary or tertiary missions such as "doing well by society")- such a powerful driver, especially with government's prompting, and especially with their competitors making that profit whether they did or not!

So why did things start snowballing into an economic disaster? Because the simple, previously-developed lending standard was modified without careful consideration, because government waded in offering a newly created **right** to even those who couldn't afford it- "to have as nice a home as they want". Motherhood and apple pie ran rampant. Because those who couldn't afford it said, well if government "sez" so, and the lenders offer so, then why worry. This is America, this is my **RIGHT**. And because the lenders looked at the immediate bottom line of the government ukase, and forgot to really look at the life-threat to their companies, thinking oh well, look at how much we are making. Pretty obvious-short-term, stage-one thinking (thank you, Thomas Sowell).

And by the way, the various agencies designed to provide an assurance, whose market function was covering these loans against default, these guys also got carried away with government edict and said let's make some money by supporting these less-than-safe (toxic) loans because the government "sez" so. Well surprise, when interest rates climbed, the number and amount of insured loans that began defaulting far exceeded the capitalized amounts of the insurers.

"Wham, bam, thank you, m'am- if you don't like it, I don't give a damn."

This baby took on a life of its own, the premise of the Hazlitt Theory. Started with intervention, grew with lack of foresight, prospered with greed, and then caved. So there is the cause-celeb, with solutions forth-coming. Where did this mess go wrong? I think the Fed Watch Dog did not do things correctly. I think that Fannie Mae and Freddie Mac didn't do their due diligence adequately, although they may have tried but been over-ridden. I think the Congress and the White House did not listen to their staffers. I think that private enterprise's top management did not steer their companies correctly with an eye to the future. I think that individual borrowers sublimated fears and the warnings proffered with each loan application, with the strong desire for fulfilling a dream. I think these borrowers didn't have a chance, although their education and innate intelligence should have triggered internal warnings that you don't get something for nothing (in this case, they did get loans but what an attendant risk!); they were too gullible after having embraced prophecies about the future. Note that every investment product to be sold clearly states "past performance is no indication of future behavior".

And then we got "Big Brother & Company", those wonderful movers and shakers that allowed this thing to initiate, fester, and become a major chancre, now with panic in their hearts, and only short-term understanding in their minds. Look at what was offered- a giant dose of further intervention. We have a massive break in the dike, and someone's got a lot of bubble gum to fill it.
Time to step back and re-examine basics. Look at our country and start planning based on the premises that founded it. Also, since we are a global economy we need to expand our model. Modern western civilization is supposed to operate on the premise of moral actions by moral people, and on the premise that government's purpose is the protection of people's rights. The mechanisms in place in our society actually do foster free market interactions, the only issue is with the value system we use during interactions. Time to dig ourselves out of this economic chasm we have created.

At the time of this writing, our new administration is attempting to wrestle with two big trends that have major impact on our country. With a lock on both congressional houses, and a president of the same mindset, it is interesting to find that a shoe-in is not obvious. The first issue is the concept of "health-care" that used to be called "health insurance'. Simple word change that completely redefined the idea and took it from assuring solvency to assuring coverage. There is a moral quandary to consider, the consideration that each of us is our brother's keeper. I personally look at it that each of us can offer what is felt to be morally responsible, and that is through some form of charity; but not that each of us is required by law to translate our own capabilities into support for someone else. That may sound harsh, but in reality each of us makes our own way from childhood to adult, and must recognize that his/her own capabilities must be translated into the ability to live as one would desire. Hard work, education, smarts- these things point the direction towards a good life. Education is a key, because here if anywhere, is a road to molding your talents into useable commodities.

There is also the consideration of when "America First" might take on an air of protectionism. A basic premise of the tax change is that lower taxes mean that companies can be more competitive in the market place. That is one prong. Another is consideration of tariffs to equalize the manufacturing playing field. EVERYTHING MUST BE RECOGNIZED AS TRANSITIONAL. In that I mean that if tariffs cause imports to equal home-grown prices, then surely retribution by the foreign source will occur. So as a transitional possibility, American companies MUST create business plans that take tax reduction on the one hand, tariffs on the other, and uses these factors to REDUCE their costs. This will allow the tariff to phase away and eventually let all businesses compete on a world playing field. The lower tax brackets will be the cause for maintaining price reductions.

So what I've said so far can be part of a foundation for this effort, it offers some sort of guidance towards resolution. Let's take a look at specific issues that are obvious contributory shortfalls in our system, and apply some system analysis towards developing corrective actions. That is what the following chapters offer.

ARTICLE 4   LOOKING TO THE LIGHT AND LESSONS TO BE LEARNED

We need to examine the trends in this country, and see whether socialism or capitalism offers the appropriate societal bent.

Let's get a <u>Mission Statement</u>:
In today's global, technological economy, the societies of Man are a world-wide amalgam. Note that I am talking about those societies that are global in thinking, and are rational in action. They are the baselines of modern civilization, the ladders for achievement. The formations within these societal structures allow movement, development, growth, and "sustainment" of the individual. The societies are based on the market concept, allowing anyone to produce (or their product will be replaced by some other producer's- so find your own niche); and the government concept, which operates as a voluntary subscription for protection of property. **Therefore; it is required that a self-correcting and self-sustaining societal mechanism be maintained that will allow individuals to achieve their full potential, without the coercion of others.**

And next a limited list of <u>Objectives</u>, germane at least, to this effort:
- Establish an inherent monetary oversight methodology that allows moral, universal, commercial activity and ensures societal economic health
- Towards the example of free enterprise in action, and in support of individualism and privatization, continue the development of a health-care methodology that offers availability of services as required by any, on a free market basis
- Insure and maintain a government charter based on protecting the rights of the individual but not infringing through control

The <u>Values</u> under which this inquiry will be conducted:

- Property- consisting of life, physical possessions, and intellectual possessions, is to be respected and protected as belonging to the individual
- Morality-interactions will consist of "right actions" (true and valid) that do not affect the property of another without his consent.

<u>Premises</u> for this effort:

- There is no inalienable right to wealth
- There is no right to free food, housing, or health care
- There is no right to the possessions of others
- There is no right to a job, only the right to apply for one and be selected based on competence and capability
- There is no right to happiness, only the right to pursue it
- Charity can be offered by anyone, but nothing can be taken from anyone against their will

The <u>Analysis</u>:

First the FINANCIAL CRISIS: what we will look at is what happened, what was done, and the lessons learned.

Any concept of a bail-out is really a cop-out concept, in spite of the fact that it may be helpful to some degree. It handles symptoms, not source. It has two components, one aimed at shoring up floundering institutions, and then shoring up of the floundering general consumer. Neither of these components supports individualism or the free market concept.

Look at the industries that have been selected for support- mortgage, banking, the automotive industry, insurance and regulatory agencies associated with it. These have been selected because they are the largest and most easily targeted institutions for support. But, as a consequence of this initial crunch, many major retailers have also been severely affected. Unfortunately, wasn't this effect actually the free market at work? And if some are selected for support, which and why? Shouldn't this be the risk/reward concept, the investment/gamble concept, upon which all endeavors are based?

Shouldn't this be "nothing ventured, nothing gained" to the epitome. Business reversal is a constant and ever-existing potential in private industry. How much reserve and what back-ups are placed into future planning is a factor that defines prudence in management. It is risk management. The large corporations, their executives, and the large numbers of personnel whose very job is managing the company's future (staff whose job it is to assess such risk and propose mitigation), are all required in their very job description to pay attention to new and marginal ventures. As this goes for private industry, it also applies to current government oversight/regulation. For the companies, this is part of their bread and butter, and when the venture collapses, the consequences are there, period. For the government, this is where the concept of protecting the rights of the citizen comes into play. No fine line here, just a hard recognition that screwing up the world's financial operations will damage everyone's peace of mind and their current and future plans as well, this is part of the high level of job responsibility placed on the government.

The failures are strictly the consequence of poor management- both on the part of private industry and on the part of government and its oversight function. The failures can be divided into a triad of "P's": policy, procedure, and personnel. Policies and procedures are the brain-children of personnel. Thus, the most important of these, the part that makes the main difference, is failure by elected and appointed personnel to set proper standards. Here I am talking about the leadership that let this slide to where it went. They either did not know, did not listen, did not care, OR WORSE-WANTED THIS TO HAPPEN. (That covers the gamut of possibilities). But it no longer matters about placing blame, at this time what matters is correction. And correction needs be a multi-faceted endeavor along a path of recovery. So again, transition becomes a major player as the time line progresses towards solution.

Let's talk about any bail-out- it is an interim attempt at containment of damage. What are we "bailing out" and why are we doing it? What we are really doing is disconnecting action from consequence- that's what is being bailed out; the connection is being severed. This bail out will contain codicils, and rightly so, since money will be given and there needs to be protection thereof for the investment or infusion. The conditions must contain a requirement for major revision in the policies and procedures of the primary affected organizations so that a moral risk-aware management mind-set is truly implemented.

One of the questions will be whether or not current management, them-there guys that allowed us to get here, are the right people to guide us out. I hate to say it, but I think not. And my reasoning is exactly why top management deserves big bonuses and salaries when they take the positions, because the positions are worth it!! If management screws up, and I mean even once, then they were bad choices for the positions, and because the management contracts did not include "punitives"- then these guys deserve to be severed, because that is the recourse they willingly signed up for. Let it be a lesson to the big corporation, and to government: bonuses can and should be negative as well. It's the old reap and sow thing.

Well, that is not all there is to discuss about this subject, as a matter of fact, it is a diversion of focus.

Let's get back to the meat of the matter, which is companies in trouble, both the directly and indirectly affected. Even bankruptcy doesn't really make it, because it leaves one heck of a lot of subsidiary companies, industry-related companies, and investors in trouble when debts are forgiven or reduced. So the ripple flows along and gets everyone, since economies are simply the business interactions of the participants (thanks again, Mr. Hazlitt). I don't know all the details of what would have been the best way to recover our economy. I have no problem with government coming up with a plan, since it is one of the biggest financial giants. But it must be a plan that can stand against other solutions based on being in competition with combined sectors within the free market working together to take over and correct troubled paths. There must remain the concept and practice of the free market, with all its wide fluctuations, as basically being the natural way of interaction. So if the government wants to help, then it does so simply as an investor, and between the affected companies and this investor, the bonds of an agreement must be struck. But there is one basic part that is essential- it is not the charter of government to run these corporations, it is not the charter of government to invest in these corporations, and it is not the charter of government to penalize these companies. It is the charter of government to protect the rights of citizens, and when the basic structure of society is challenged by a potential financial melt-down, then and then only, government and/or sectors of the economy can vie for offering solutions. Profit will always be considered as a by-product, even government makes one in the offering of bonds, t-bills, etc. and in getting quality personnel to operate it. By the way, profit is absolutely not a dirty word. It is the basis for all interactions. Profit is measured as increase in happiness, security, or finances.

But now, to discuss the oversight function that is necessary to guide our monetary system in such a manner that this big a swing, this big an impact, can be anticipated and prevented. Guess what? We really already have it, it just worked poorly. What is missing is moral and fiscal authority and trigger points, and in this case, on a totally proprietary bias. Treat the fiscal economy as an entity. The oversight activity needs to be associated with the concept of proprietary guidance imbedded within results, meaning in this case placing the authority in the hands of the selected management who receive recompense proportionate to worth and results, both positive and negative. The only thing to add is morality as a part of any mission statement. Darn right it sounds simple.

Second, HEALTH-PROTECTION:
Let's start this discussion with delineation between Health Insurance and Health Care. Health Insurance is akin to Auto Insurance in that you buy a probability of need. It is based on actuarial factors that have placed each individual into a category and determined the probability through a mathematical representation that the "group" will consume some kind of average payout over the coverage time. It essentially says that there will be minimal preventative maintenance, and that usage is upon a need basis.
Health Care is not at all the same thing, because now each individual is premised to require delivered service and that this service will be provided. In other words, go in for your shots, get your teeth cleaned and your toenails trimmed, let's take an X-ray and see if

either your lassaize-faire attitude or your complaint may have any merit.

So in either case, health protection is not for free, that's the first thing that needs to be stated. The reason is simple-food, clothing, shelter. No one is owed those things, only the right to obtain them morally. Everyone needs to be a contributor of their own worth to translate that worth into a sellable commodity that will allow them to receive the wherewithal to live. Can everyone make a living? In our society, there are so many needs to be fulfilled for it to run properly, that there is always room for talents of so many varieties and capabilities to satisfy the empty slots. Everyone can aspire, it all starts with humble beginnings and a climb up the ladder. How far you go is up to your use of your talents based on your capabilities. And there is every reason to believe that as each of us adjusts our sights to *achievable reality*: so shall they achieve. In the biggest picture, if you can't reach your pinnacle at this time, it can happen later if you have the ability and if you persevere. And for those who cannot work due to bona-fide limitations, society offers a safety net of minimal support, either through charity or pared down (hopefully) "revised support" programs. (More about that later in the article on Humanitarianism.)

Back to health protection- it is not a given inalienable right. It is an "availability" in health insurance, and a selected program in health care. And neither is it at all free, each has an expense associated with it. When government takes from each of us and then redistributes by supporting programs that may or may not be within our own desire to support, that is a violation of basic moral rights. Each of us has translated our abilities into a commodity (money) that we then convert into our own accumulator of good things. One of these translations is charity, the privilege we have of giving through our own agreement. But charity has unfortunately been bastardized and modified into taxation and redistribution, and that is a violation of basic tenets of a free society. After all, that concept easily extends into how about food, clothing and shelter to any who need, as well as health care, and oh by the way, how about transportation, how about the NEED for recreational relief, ad-nausea? No argument that there will be some persons unable to cope with daily life, and these people may need support.

I am not saying no to these factors. In the free market system, there exists a vehicle for handling them. For health protection, it ranges from insurance to care, it is the crafting of a package of private enterprise initiatives that contain caps, limits, and terms that can be purchased by any consumer, at a price that provides a marginal profit to the companies, and limited, selectable, but sufficient services to the purchaser. No different than auto insurance, life insurance, basically any kind of insurance. Minimum standards assure that sub-marginal companies and their offerings would not remain long in the market place, because no one would buy a deficient product, and these would either morph or fail.

And third, GOVERNMENT FOCUS: On protecting the rights of citizens rather than becoming the business that supplies them:
Big Brother sounds so easy, but as Orwell offered, comes with some pretty heavy threats to freedom. First issue to consider is the current staffing of the federal government. Sure, all government functions operate, but a key set of hierarchical questions needs to be asked.

1. Is the function rightly placed within the definition of government, ie.... protecting the rights of the citizen?
2. Does the operational entity provide a useful and necessary function?
3. Is there a private industry alternative either available or in place, one that offers higher efficiency? One of the things of note is that in private industry if budget over-runs, there will be a come-uppance, while in government service there is a tax or fee increase.
4. If there is not a private industry alternative at this time, would one make sense? Is there expertise to operate it? Would it be less expensive?

Probably there are more questions to ask, but with those above, we have a start at identifying un-necessary or improper government functionality. But be wary, this evaluation is critical and cannot be allowed to become political. One of the easiest ways to begin this process is simply to reduce the budgets of all government functions. This would be done after a validation and redefinition of the functions and responsibilities of each of the organizations. This combination would establish a charter, and then a mechanism of paring chaff. It would not eliminate function, simply streamline it. The next step would be the questioning of private vs. government sponsorship of the function. Transfer to private industry would require the development of a transition plan. It could include utilizing some of the expertise that exists in the positions now. By the way, what I am describing is what happens in private industry after every merger, after every management change, and after each revision in corporate goals.

There is a maxim that has always been around, that "security is the lowest form of human happiness". Once upon a time that maxim applied to government positions, not the best paying, but for sure, secure in that few got fired except for exceptional cause. Now however, government jobs are on an equal footing with private industry, with a skewed set of standards away from free enterprise, yet equally competitive in remuneration. Well, if that is true, then not only should government function compete for talent, it should compete for marketplace position (if it has as a goal the entry into the marketplace). Bigness is no longer a reason for awarding the job function, there are many large corporations or combinations thereof that could easily handle market niche. Is this heresy? Not in my opinion, especially if private industry can demonstrate ability to satisfy the requirements of the function. And, a careful paring needs to be accomplished to insure that the function is not bloated or overloaded with non-essentials, both in functionality and in personnel. As well, it is essential to insure that budgeting recognizes limits, that in fact there cannot be a return to the till without recognizing and correcting bloat, inefficiency, and requirements creep.

Government has grown, too large now, because it is too easy to let any purview that uses the public coffers to slip into that vein. Due to the nature of democracy, it is a long process to implement change. That is why it is necessary to get back to basics and establish a long-term plan that has gone through the critical thinking necessary to ensure rightness in approach.

So where are we after all this discussion? I believe that the answer is that people need time to digest, and then begin a grass roots dialogue that will produce a process leading into transition planning. I believe this should not be done rapidly, it requires a lot of churning, both of stomach and of mind, with a really strong dose of emotion. I for one am quite ready for this dialogue, it has done a lot of its churning inside of me for quite a while now.

And fourth as a direct follow-on to 3 above, focus on Foreign Policy and Diplomacy: our government as the spokesperson and director for us abroad. That's what we want when we elect an administration, we put our all into the belief that they will populate with persons satisfying what we wanted and elected them to portray. So we need to understand whether our selectees are in fact following what they promised when elected, and which ostensibly represents our desires. After all, we live in a big world where we do not control anything other than ourselves, and that not very well, note that we do not even really control our own destiny.

In the realm of foreign affairs, once we were insular, and that because travel was tedious and communication was slow. But in today's world, everything is wide open and some things instantaneous. That really opened the door to world-trade and a new outlook on global economics. But we never forget that we derived from the animal kingdom, and so in additional to mutual benefit, we see posturing and domination grow their ugly heads. We need to look at what diplomacy is all about, because therein lies a path towards peaceful co-existence. In its simplest form, diplomacy is the art of the deal, the fulfillment of the desire to do well by improving and cementing relations. How we go about doing that is based on the representatives allowed to speak for our country. Policy starts at home in the minds of the policy-makers, and is supposedly based on obtaining the best for the constituents. But the constituents are a mass of people, a mass of minds and ideas, of desires and agendas, and conflicting opinions. So although the representatives of the people were selected through lawful process, they could easily represent less than 50% of the desires of the people, and it's almost a guarantee that that is the case. So let's look at the various world conditions that need to be dealt with. They can be categorized- trade (of culture, commodities, and manufactured goods), military presence/protection, travel, political pacts, immigration, "human rights", environmental impacts, national boundaries, national goals. All of these items bring about financial expenditure and potential conflict of interest. By the way, all of these factors can be brought into domestic perspective as well, and really the foreign perspective is just an outgrowth of the home-grown mind-set. So the job of government in this very large, important, and expansive charter, is to pull together a cohesive whole that places our country into a safe amalgam. There certainly are several approaches to handling this task, but there is always a problem of the other 49% that may not agree with direction taken. What to do? That is what the election cycle is all about, every four years we can "ping-pong" again. Unhappiness expressed in the polls is the lawful way of screaming and yelling. But democracy takes years to flow smoothly back and forth in order to stabilize, or to bounce about in utter abandon, as I see it doing. I am not privy to all the machinations or all the facts of the international community, therefore my criticisms and comments cannot truly reflect reality, they only reflect my own perceptions. But I do know that the august United Nations body, which founding intent was to present a unified global view and a forum to so obtain, has not lived up to expectations. It has become a forum, but of a nationalistic bent, of a very cabalistic bent, and differing from the standard definition of a forum, in that agendas are promulgated. Within this arena our government has had to stiffen resolve and backpedal on the concept of world-togetherness. The previous administration wanted to bring lofty goals down to ground-level, to modify perception and make everybody an equal, with equal say. (BY the way, that is what the General Assembly is for). And the thought is right, if it had been dealing with proper representation. But it was and is not so, in that agendas abound and every vacuum becomes filled almost as soon as previous responsibility is vacated. This administration is promulgating the concept of "America First", not a bad idea in terms of short-term recognition of a goal, but somewhat missing the point in terms of global thinking. So is there something wrong with the concept or can extended articulation boost understanding? "First" in this case means "best for", it does not mean exclusive. Winning a battle is not good enough if you lose the war, which means look ahead at the long term goals, not just the immediacy of the moment. Crafting and navigating a long term strategy is one of first setting-basic-unequivocal factors in a mission statement. Once these are firmly in front of your face, you can translate down into all the aspects that lead to a programmatic perspective and eventually to actions.

So as an example, would tariffs make sense? Their purpose is protection, and that ties into of what, and for what intent. With the new tax laws in process, the reduction of corporate tax has the three benefits of bringing business back to this country by offering tax incentive to return, of allowing for increased profit, investment, and expansion, and reducing consumer prices. But with a tariff in place threatening imports, then pricing reduction by corporations need not be as deep. So then tariffs should only be in place to offer temporary protection and to allow corporations to establish new cost structure and improved processes. Careful examination and understanding of world conditions would recognize that reciprocity is a fact of life, that threatening someone brings retaliation.
I covered some of this in my first book, "Things of Concern", not only by pointing out short-falls, but as well offering resolutions to issues and problems. I will not repeat them here, but suggest looking at that book if you are interested in my recommendations.

Figure 2   New Brighton- Simplicity

ARTICLE 5   MORE ON HEALTH CARE AND GOVERNMENT

This country was founded on the concept of freedom of the individual; and our government was formed, as the definition offers, strictly to support and protect the freedom of its citizens. So it is very disturbing when I see BIG government setting itself up to enter the private enterprise realm. This is NOT what free enterprise is about, nor is it commensurate with the ideas that make America great.

I am speaking in this instance strictly about Health Care. The free enterprise system, as well as democracy, cycles with changes in conditions, and the system essentially learns through the corrective process, finally resulting in the workable commodity. That means that private industry needs to re-look and modify its offerings, such as packages of health care insurance that are affordable and offer adequate coverage. This does not mean that the government, which is funded by tax dollars, should go into competition with private enterprise to offer health care, knowing that if it needs to, the government will simply reach into the tax coffers to shore up any shortfalls. This is anathema to the concept of free enterprise.

If some of the people elect not to have coverage because they feel they don't get very sick very often, that is a choice. If some of the people elect not to have coverage because they have more important things to spend money on, that is OK. Those who feel they need certain kinds of coverage can band together as a pressure group to sway the insurance industry into offering a less expensive or more appropriate package. The insurance companies welcome the challenge of opening up new markets.

If part of the cost of a package is the price of doctors, or the threat of lawsuit, or the cost of prescriptions, then competition should handle it. NOT GOVERNMENT, not my tax dollar subsidy. Cutting costs is always better than increasing subsidy or price.

So mechanisms need to be in place to support health care change within the free enterprise system, not the establishment of a socialistic America.

We are a trading society, and what that means is that we seek what we want, and offer what someone else wants, and when they meet, you have a deal.

But let's also look at individual health care needs. These fall into six categories- general check-ups, preventative care, specific injuries, emergencies, recoveries, long-term palliative care. And the choices for program funding to handle these needs can be essentially defined as "you–pay (all by yourself)", "we-pay (you and society)", "someone-else-pays (not you)". How can programs be set up to satisfy the health care "needs-categories" and assure that only the required care is funded, and that the optional items (which could be considered by some as necessary, by others as desired but not required) are available, but not mandatory, and therefore the funding is commensurate with the degree to which a recipient is willing to support it? Get those insurance companies to develop plans and recommend them.

Equally as interesting are the subjects of second-opinions and monopolies. They do tie in to each other in that checks and balances are in both realms- in the case of a second opinion it means that another separate source has something to say, while in the monopolistic realm it means there is no second source. Careful consideration of second opinions is necessary, and oversight is critical to assure that in all cases, even monopoly, that true and valid inputs are available. There can be no rules that say "only this" will be considered, or that "we insist you push this solution". Yet, whether it is private industry or government single-source, these possibilities exist and must be checked. In private industry, there is always another opinion that can be obtained, in single-source, although there may be multiple opinions, the rules must allow for such judgements. And that is really the only way that expert opinion can be evaluated, because even experts have predisposed inclinations.

Hard to believe, but in system engineering, this very question is a perfect candidate for a full blown trade-off study that can offer choices for decision based on firm requirements and the decision parameters selected as Measures of Merit. So let's do it! And let's do it based on setting up requirements for a program and then a resolution matrix. Rather than imbedding this study within this one small section of this manuscript, I have placed the study as ADDENDUM 1 at the end of the book (page 69).

Well, have you read ADDENDUM 1 and looked at its miniscule and abbreviated Problem Resolution Study? You needn't reach the same conclusion as I have, you needn't even agree with my choice of parameters, measures of merit, or logic. Think about it yourself, and eradicate my flaws and replace them with your truths.

Now what do you think?

ARTICLE 6   HUMANITARIANISM

In discussing free enterprise and free choice, with all that I have been saying so far, and with the bent that is apparent in my writing and thinking, I feel that it is necessary to devote a section to my feelings on supporting those who need help living life. Presently, there are two avenues offering support, one being charitable considerations, the other being government support.

To start, each of us must look inside and feel comfortable with our own moral standards. As we each embrace our day and our fate, and move along our path, there needs to be recognition that not everyone can follow quite an equivalent path- some because of mental conditions, some because of circumstance of birth, or inability to tap into educational standards required, or the disasters of illness, finances, or essentially any situation that might require support for extrication.

I have mentioned "charitable consideration", and the concept of charity, and now I would like to offer an expanded definition. Charity is derived from what your own energy has produced in terms of affluence, it is the faceless attribute of money placed into a pool that serves what you consider a righteous cause (of which the above offers examples), and it has to clearly fit in with your own moral definitions. This "charity" can take two forms; the first being investment and the second being safety net. In the concept of investment, what is proffered will result in a bootstrapping effect in that it offers help to those who strive to rise, and when they do, they provide society with a positive result. In the concept of safety net, there are the categories wherein there will be no rise, merely subsistence. Both of these describe conditions of humanity, both must be recognized as realities, and any society must ingrain methodology to meet the needs of such individuals and their condition.

People are not necessarily obliged, but rather can be motivated, to look at charitable conditions and respond. And it is education within society, whether at home, peers, school-initiated education, or religious belief that defines and then supports this category. But unfortunately, human nature offers that there will be those who wish to take unfair advantage of any opportunity. Therefore a category must be well defined so that the moral person accepts that those within it are bona-fide. With that as a starting point, and moral education as a *given* for all people, then there will be support offered to fill the necessities of the truly needy. This support can come from voluntary contributions for either investment or subsistence, and can then be directed either towards the "investment" category or the "subsistence" group. The investment category fits well with private enterprise or entrepreneurship. Government does not really have charter to support the investment category, but does need to support the subsistence group.

So, you ask, how similar is this to welfare, how similar to student loans, how similar to other programs? The answer is that these thoughts are similar, but in looking at how they are handled and administered, I believe that today there is significant waste, significant scam. That is part of the problem with government sponsorship, it is essentially non-proprietary and purely administrative. At present it is fraught with inefficiency. In some respects, there are needs for support across the land, and here government function is certainly a reasonable consideration. But there needs to be two separate views for handling the financing of organizations supporting either category. In terms of "investment" there needs to be a return on that investment (either payback and/or the satisfaction of seeing completion), and with investment, private companies can be created to operate such programs through loan or through other entrepreneurial consideration. This has been done with student loans or scholarships for example. Categories include education through schooling with the goal of producing skills that are desirable in the marketplace, actual job training by companies needing to fill open positions, or apprenticeships. By the way, spending money on education and training is far superior to spending money to incarcerate.

In terms of subsistence programs, funding would be absolutely minimal but adequate, and such programs as highway trash pickup and other community tasks can be filled by those who have adequate ability, and this works as an investment to produce useful output. For those bona-fides unable to work, there would be no reciprocal requirements. Here the definition of government could be considered as a safety net for those citizens who cannot exist alone within our society.

The big difference between government funded and charity-driven is that the former would be a required pay-in while the latter would be a voluntary subscription. You might ask, how to assure sufficiency of funding and contributors for the latter? This is where the concept of mind-set, established throughout the country, becomes an important factor. Recognition of NIMBY would be translated into "how can I support- how to help the homeless, the mentally ill, those who need that second chance?" Education, up-bringing, and social mindedness are factors that should be promulgated throughout our society to instill in its people that such moral rightness is ingrained. After all, if a thing is government funded, it should represent the will of the people anyway, so it should rather be voluntary contribution with its attendant satisfaction. Using this concepting, the free market would generate support for those in need, and it would add a proprietary aspect to it, not only that individuals have voluntarily contributed on a personal basis, but that oversight would equally have a proprietary perspective for success based on market economics. And for any universal government-auspices program, market forces plus government obligation for minimal support will be available.

ARTICLE 7   ON TERRORISM-A SCARY REVERSAL

Here is a really scary endeavor about the approach to terrorism- the decision that the policies and procedures sanctioned and in use by an agency of the government, which had been blessed and approved by all parties and their leaderships, are now determined to be fodder for attack on those individuals to whom they applied as operational guidelines. I am talking about the methods of handling terrorists. Of course there are so many other things that fall into this category, it really depends on the political mind and its smallness that would allow such chipping away at institutions for political purposes. I don't call it cleaning house when someone turns around and begins an exercise of back-stabbing in the name of purity. That does not even remotely smack of any sense of morality or logic- it is the introduction of the witch-hunt. And that is what was done when a new administration brought in their perspective on terrorism. Once again comes the thought of fairness and moderation, compromise and appeasement, in the name of offering the feathers of the dove of peace. What is clear but not acknowledged by some, is the reality that fanaticism does not compromise, it takes and feeds. To delve into the pathways of thinking and reacting in the interest of understanding and perhaps changing, requires careful selection of method. Orwell's 1984 did it using blind terror and subtle brain-wash. Factors include time available, moral imperatives, allowable damage to the subject, cost of doing business.

The first question would be- "what ways and means are available for either developing a status quo or eliminating a threat to world peace?" How do you hold out your hand when you know darn well it will be cut off? Does this mean that bargaining will not work, or does it mean that there needs to be a change in offerings? I believe the latter is the answer, and part of the solution will be to suitably agree on goals for both sides. But getting back to the reversal, it is really about mind-set and methods. In all societies, clearly the news press is one of the leading methods of forming mind-set. Others, like education, peer pressure, the family dinner table, each has a place in the direction of the heart and mind, but when faced with a developed outlook, some are no longer appropriate.

When each of us starts out, we are really a malleable young mind, impressionably waiting for formation and guidance. Education, peer pressure, family, experiences, are the factors that come into play. As we grow and mature, we realize that society requires forms of agreement in order to function. And so come the rules and regulations. These start out at some point in time frozen and bathed in the mind-set of the day. Not only that, but the concept of the Mission to which these new rules and regulations apply should firmly be established to assure that what comes out is what was intended. Probably takes a long period of time to bring all this to fruition, and in the process, checks and balances, deals, agreements, pledges, etc… are set in place. And when it's done, it was a process that ended up getting something to completion, and the minds and mind-sets of the working personnel contributed to it. So if and when change is desired, it deserves equal mental time and exposure to insure relevancy and authenticity of thought. Not emotion, not politics, but a larger view that recognizes that this is our country and its basics that are being modified, and by all means if correction is required, then it should be thought about and eventually legislated. Comes to mind PROHIBITION, and subsequent ABOLISHMENT THEREOF. The ping-pong attitude, the vitriolic mind-set, these do not belong in the leadership role of a major government.

ARTICLE 8   I AM TOO, PROUD OF MYSELF

Everyone rationalizes their confidence about, and happiness with, themselves. We all look and pretty much see that we are doing things the way we want to, we are ostensibly moving where we want to move, and sure, we need to make adjustments in that movement if it is off-course. That is both the good and the bad of it all. But this is just a form of rationalization that allows us to pursue our current course. It has another side however, one that looks at "poor me" and acquiesces that current status is a consequence of external forces too strong to overcome. And there is the challenge to re-program more than a simple tweak, but to lay out a new direction, a new approach, a new you.   This is hard. It takes de-programming on your part as well as re-programming to fill the new void. But guess what, if you don't periodically re-examine your status, then that will remain your status. I am not saying anything that isn't obvious, but seeing it in front of you is stronger than the simple thought alone. Every form of reinforcement is a tool that is part of your arsenal, and greases the skids for movement.

Need to go to ground on this one, which is to get to basics of what makes a person tick. The de-programming is exceptionally hard if the programming was extreme and long lasting. At the base level, morals are a first order influence. Ethics are a first order influence. Critical thinking, in whatever form and manner, is major. This means really take a look at who and what you are right now; why you are what you are, and is this truly acceptable or only marginally so? The gauge is happiness; big picture happiness looks at every aspect and creates the balance sheet that tells the tale.

Respect should lay over all of this- respect for yourself, for others, for that which is called both primary and secondary property. Primary property is your life, your possessions; secondary property is your thoughts, ideas, your word, your intellect. "Ain't no more than this, baby". Each of us has naturally endowed talents and abilities, that is what we come into this world with, and as we learn to use these gifts, that is our way of moving through the world. We translate our abilities into products that we offer the rest of the world, and trade for what we need or want. We accumulate the things of need, whether simply things or intellectual support, and then we look at whether we are happy and satisfied with what we are accumulating. Of course, there is a perspective to consider, and that relates to accumulating strictly physical things. These physical things can form a baseline for you, a departure point from which you aspire to heights way beyond the physical. This is a most important aspect, because you really do need the base from which to depart on the journey. The physical part is just that, a base from which to depart.

Notice that I am taking a diversionary path for a moment - all relates, but obliquely. This has to do with personal property/intellectual property, in the form of what each of us is capable of producing. I am particularly talking about art, whether it be painting, photography, dance, sculpture, poetry, prose, physical ability (such as sports) - whatever, and the pride in the product. Each of us has to reach within to determine if we are willing to stand the exposure of allowing others to see/ comment/ criticize/approve/reject what is the deepest part of our being translated into a display. As Ruth Gordon said in "Harold and Maude"- "take a chance". Classic line, it is even more poignant than "nothing ventured, nothing gained", because the former puts you out there, the latter only speaks to effort. This is the wonder of life, it flows and the currents offer opportunity in so many directions.
And to bring this back to the major theme, you should be proud of yourself, your capabilities, and your ability to choose your own way in life.

You might ask, why this chapter? Well, throughout this book, there is a struggle apparent between individuality and socialism. And this small section offers a look at one path, that of personal movement and independence, one of confidence in your own ability to live your life, your way.

Figure 3 Twin Lakes- Profusion

ARTICLE 9   SURPRISES

As you read this manuscript, you can surely notice a sense of bias, and frankly, I have no problem with that because everyone has opinions, and they are allowed to be freely expressed everywhere. But in order for freedom of speech to really function well, champions of all sides of an issue need equal opportunity to so say. Sometimes that is hard, because opinions are deeply seated, tempers are a function of personality, and set and setting for the conditions of conversation will vary.

No doubt, we are in a very divisive political and social climate within the US at this time. We have concerns or approvals for the ways the government is handling foreign policy, the economy, entitlements, immigration, climate, trade, and the role of government itself. The past president brought his formative past with him, and supported his party to the extent of alienating many who were not as uniquely focused. Compromise was in his vocabulary, but not in his actions.

The current president has brought a completely different mind-set and background to the office. Only partially a surprise, because his propensities were obvious during the campaign, but two things bulled him through to the presidency. The first was his opposition, selected by the Democratic Caucus process, which placed a vulnerable candidate in the limelight. The second was the desire of the electorate to believe that if one candidate was flawed, the other could remake himself after the campaign and become a stalwart diplomat that would properly fill the shoes of the office; just what was wanted.

Surprise, that has not happened yet, and it is not obvious that it will happen. Apparently there are two foci, the first to continue his normal blather, the second, to try and implement some of the things on his agenda. The electorate looks on askance, even worse, a large percentage look on with (almost?) hatred. They see a man, they see a position, and they absolutely abhor that particular combination. Oh woe, this is the office of the President of the United States, and it is viewed with such acrimony that it consumes all sense of delegation that should have resulted from the election cycle. Surprise- the large minority rallying that has grown a significant opposition to change. Our culture is in the throes of change or clarification itself, and this relates to immigration, healthcare, taxation methods, business growth. All of these issues relate basically to internal social policy within the United States. Large and influential pressure groups and grass-roots causes have moved to the fore and slot well into political rhetoric. But dissention has become outright slathering, even so far that elected officials are vocally displaying disdain for process, policy, procedure, tradition. Not to mention that the past administration laid time-bombs within the laws of the land- DACA as a prime example. Utilizing Executive Authority allows the fostering of foothold, and once there, no one likes to give up anything. So now forgetting the origin, here comes "purity and motherhood". It is marching right up to the Center of Government, and demanding more and more.

I don't necessarily believe in conspiracy, but I do have a problem with so much lining up to thwart any actions undertaken by an administration. To me it is clear that every "chad" hanging is another opportunity to discredit. I guess I am surprised that this is so vitriolic. When I think about it, I see three things that are in the target zone. The first is still the loss by Hillary, the second is the personality of the current president, the third is the policies of this current administration. When I drill down, the Hillary loss is more about not getting into power when they were there, more than about the individual. Too much manipulation, too much potential for "pay to play", and when it was realized, it was too late, and so the loss is strictly on the party choice, and what that did to focus. And as a consequence, anything, small or dirty or compromising, is all fair game for getting even. As far as personality, no doubt that Trump is a different kind of person than would normally fit the presidential bill. He brings all his own baggage, and I consider it that way as opposed to his history and background, because in that office, there is a firm requirement to represent and protect the country. I believe he is trying, and using his past experience as the pathway for negotiation, and I believe that given time, he may in fact learn how to fulfill his obligations. But until then, if it ever happens, we have a very slippery slope to transcend. As far as policy goes, the two parties do not agree on anything. Each has backed itself into a now predictable MO- deviation from that ticket will cause party disunity, which it has, and severe acrimony among the faithful. In addition, the tides are rolling sadly into a major split in the essential requirement of the parties, and that requirement is to carry on for the good of the country.

What does the good of the country mean? Ask different people, get that many different answers. That is the nature of humankind, to see things from a personal perspective. But in the case of a united country, the criteria still remains the protection of citizen's rights to life, liberty, and the pursuit of happiness, (so long as there is no infringement on the rights and property of others).

ARTICLE 10   BUDGETS, DEFICITS, AND IOU'S

We are in the throes of financial disaster, waiting for it to happen. This applies to the federal government, the state governments, and the city and township governments. Debt ceiling increases have been used ad infinitum as a means of avoidance, until finally these ceilings represent such a large proportion of our GNP that we are rapidly working our way to insolvency. Everyone looks and says NIMBY, let it pass on to the next generation. At least that is so on the federal level. On the California state level, we are not too far behind, except that we are seriously in the abysmal and losing throes of cutting back on expenses through wage and perk negotiations on reduced hours and furloughs on other services, yet increasing minimum wage which influences all costs. Same with the cities, and with the townships. But what I see is posturing as well as limited action.

Everyone understands that retirement pensions have increasingly impinged on budgets. And part of the reason is that investments are not offering expected growth, and speculation as opposed to investment is too dangerous. The continuous demand on pensions by those already retired and those aspiring, is beyond the funding capability available. The commitments have brought such pensions into the 25% or more budget range. This has meant higher taxes and fees in order to meet the needs of these commitments. And typically, instead of cutting back, there is more demand for increased budget, more demand on the spendable income of the citizen whose taxes have continuously increased. But pensions are only one piece of the problem. Reducing unnecessary expense is not in the mind-set, only deliberately picking necessities as candidates for removal, things that we cannot downgrade. (That'll show 'em!!)

A new tax code is here. As I see it, it has both pluses and minuses. In the biggest of pictures, corporate taxes go down and if correctly applied, the largesse can be used to do two main things- reduce prices, and allow expansion with its concurrent job growth. Some portion will obviously be taken for profit increase, but that is human and corporate nature. In the smallest of pictures, I believe that everyone should end up with a tax reduction, no matter who you are.

This all banks on the expansion of markets that should result from the reduction in pricing from the reduction in taxation. (By the way, tariffs can be applied but oh woe, they have their own problems.) Will it happen this way? History implies yes in the long term, logic states yes, but there is still an issue.

Some of the government functions have crept in and up beyond the charter of STRICTLY "protection of life, liberty and the ability to pursue happiness" (but none at the expense of others without their consent). So there needs to be a careful look at all of these areas. Amazing, we actually had a government shut-down for a few days this month (January, 2018), and when all the government departments were asked for their contingency plans, the output was mind-blowing. The question was to what level would you pare your staffs until the shut-down was resolved? And the lists offered was amazing: from 3800 down to 300, from 1000 down to 7 as two examples. But that's only two examples, and of course, these are exceptional extremes. In reality, the paring process in response to how to save money on salaries would be less dramatic, because staying open with almost no output is not the same as functioning well and permanently as an agency.

To handle debt limit, T-bills and bonds and other instruments are all promises to pay in return for up-front loan. Dependent on the interest rate and maturity offered, these loans double or triple the amount owed at completion. And of course, in many instances, the due dates are far enough in the future, that little thought is given to the come-uppance. In the business world, these things seriously affect the evaluation of the company. Our government is a company, and budget deficits, loans, future obligations, all influence the credibility and viability of our country and how it is run. Not good.

ARTICLE 11   TERRORIST MIND-SET

Two possibilities- either hatred or blind fanaticism, maybe both linked one to the other through indoctrination. Is fanaticism blind? I believe so, because all other forces are over-ridden. I cannot really analyze this correctly because I have never experienced it. That does not mean I don't have a mind-set, but what it does mean is that my logical mind has tempered any hard line positions with some form of rationale, and this, much to my chagrin.   The concept of rightness is a big factor in a person's drive, and unfortunately, what I call indoctrination is not seen that way by everyone. So it comes down to delving within and ascertaining whether there are (or should be) some basic rules for people living together.

This is not an easy thing to accomplish, because the basic drives of differing cultures set the ground rules for interaction. But BREAKTHROUGH- it can get back to the basic concept of property. Here is the least common denominator. Everyone is attached to their ideology, (which by definition, is right for them), and *that* idea is key to the concept of property as well. If you have read any of my other books, you have found that I consider respect for property to be a lynch-pin in dealing with other people.

So let's go back to a beginning- the Mid-East. Here is where ping-pong sounds like the best description, except it is with lives, not tiny little balls. Areas that stick out like sore thumbs are Jerusalem, all of Israel, IsiS/IsiL, Iran, Syria, Afghanistan, Nigeria, not necessarily in that order, but all are fomenting messes. Reminds me of an Oscar Brown Jr. song- "Forty Acres and a Mule". That was about slavery and the promise that recompense would consist of those items. But in the mid-east, the ante is much higher and the conflict no less deep. It's about deserving, and is that appropriate? Also about downright hatred and need to hurt, not even about restitution.   Witness what happened when Gaza went to the Palestinian State and the first thing the Palestinians did was tear down anything left by the Israelis, and that included buildings and infrastructure because they were built with Israeli hands.   The question of deserving is not an easy one to handle. Stepping back, you can ask who is it that should do the restitution to the so-called "deserving"? There probably are layers of involvement; finger-pointing is the child's way of getting there.

Every act that led up to the "deserving" status is part of the daisy chain that got there. Here is the concept of property taken to an extreme, because instead of rationality, there is only emotion. Is history the correct perspective for claims, or is it to the conqueror goes the spoils- but somewhere there needs to be a solution, and guess what, it is waiting to be found.

Of course there is another issue to contend with, and that is that insular behavior requires rejection of any invasiveness. That is directly applicable to extreme Muslim fundamentalism and the threat that any other belief poses to that position. Not only any belief, but also the benefits of an educated populace, one that sees the rest of the world, and can question. That flies in the face of indoctrination. It is premised that anything other is "enemy", one opposed to the way things are, and the interpretation imposes a need to eliminate any such threat. The belief in God, the interpretation by the Prophet, and the understanding of the holy Koran have been placed inside an interpreted box, and premise acceptability, nay, requires, the use of violence, to remove opposition. I wrote about this in my book, "Things of Concern", and have looked at the forms for finding a peaceful solution to such an aggressive position. Any ideology that refuses to look for diplomatic solution is one that needs to be truly boxed or eliminated. So that infers "eye for an eye", but yet, can also be resolved by allowing lines to be drawn if both parties are willing. Unfortunately, it is exactly this thinking that is the backbone of the terrorist, to gain and then flaunt the gain and go for more. No end, because terrorism is an affront on property, it requires concession that means eventually giving up. Terrorism is theft, because it takes and destroys what belongs to someone else. Can there be an isolationist policy that works? I think so, but it must be not only diplomatic and geographic, but military in nature to assure that further inroads do not break any status quo.

Do we all see that terrorism is a deadly game that is not acceptable? Its proponents take away your property by causing unproductive expenditure to combat it as well as any physical take-over of your property, it takes your property by destroying it, it takes property by killing innocent people, it takes your (mind) property by subjugation.

It **is** the loudest protest possible, but it goes beyond civilized bounds. When I see it in that light, it makes me realize that terrorism does not belong within modern civilizations, because it is a destroyer, never a builder. Even its goals are destructive- to foster a non-compromising view of the world, to convert through force the ideal of freedom of choice into one of required acceptance of a different world view. Terrorism has roots, and these can be from different sources. Religious zeal is acceptable and proselytizing can be condoned, so long as there is choice, but not in a threatening, destructive manner.

How to change that? Long term solution would include education rather than brain-washing, with the goals to develop respect for all beings and their ideas, ideals, property, thoughts, life. It must start at the youngest of ages, and for those already indoctrinated, it must include a revision and thoroughly different view of life.

ARTICLE 12   IMMIGRATION

Touchy subject, eh? I have spoken about this before, and didn't want to really get into it again. BUT. It's not a hard thing to handle. Both Democrats and Republicans have some rightness on their sides, because this is an interesting dilemma obviously with which we as a country have a history. So here's the thing: we are a sovereign nation, and that comes first because morality, which is a component, even though absolute, is not seen that way by large groups of people. What that means is that we have the right, within our borders, to control requests for entry. A border goes along by definition with sovereign territory, and this border's purpose is to give time for our own cogitation before acts are performed. For the migrant or potential immigrant, crossing that border is really crossing a line-new authority is in place.

The components of the immigration issue are tri-fold: moral, lawful, physical:

- The moral component of immigration is the first aspect that governs the others. This country was founded on the principle that the country can accept those who truly desire to come here to better their conditions. The tired, the hungry, the poor- those are what Lady Liberty speaks to. The concept has not changed, we in this country are so fortunate to have so much opportunity, and we are certainly willing to share it and help it blossom. But the moral component must then be brought into a sense of reality wherein there are acceptable methods of allowing immigrants to enter and apply for citizenship or work permits.
  - Part of the moral component is the recognition that when a person is able to establish a life presence over a period of time, then this is truly an inroad. What I mean is that if you have settled for a significant period, then you are here. That is what life is all about- surrounding yourself with your own awareness and environment. We all do it. We buy our home, we plant our shrubs, our kids go to school. And so, if through selective neglect (on the part of the executive

branch that is chartered to remove illegality, one way or another, if people have reached a point of comfort and are leading moral lives themselves, then the United States is complicit in allowing this to have occurred. Here is where morality is truly required in the recognition of complicity.

    o   Teddy Roosevelt offered some thoughts on the morality associated with the mindset of the immigrant[5].

          ▪   He said "In the first place, we should insist that if the immigrant who comes here IN GOOD FAITH, becomes an American and assimilates himself to us, he shall be treated on an exact equality with everyone else, for it is an outrage to discriminate against any such man because of creed, or birthplace, or origin. But this is predicated upon the person's becoming in every fact an American, and nothing but an American. There can be no divided allegiance here. Any man who says he is an American, but something else also, isn't an American at all. We have room for but one flag, the American flag. We have room for but one language here, and that is the English language. And we have room for but one sole loyalty and that is a loyalty to the American people."

          ▪   The other side of that coin is that a person to be so considered must operate through rules of law established by the country.

• The physical aspects relate to sovereignty assurance. Boundaries are set, and typically set for a reason, to differentiate between things, in this case areas within the United States of America versus anything outside. Such boundaries are either physically real (a wall or patrolled border) or physical/intellectually real (a visa or permit or green card). They are established to offer methodology to enforce compliance. Sometimes they are not sufficient to do the entire job because for every thing there is an opposite, and circumventing the physical barriers is sometimes a reality. But a physical barrier is appropriate if porosity is overwhelming and entry of anyone with any intent is not controlled. This applies to those who harbor ill-will as well as those who just think that they deserve to come here ahead of the legally-fostered process.

- The legal aspect speaks to defining the nature of immigration, the methods used, the limits established, the punitive effects.
    - o There needs to be some form of guidelines or rules to bound any subject. In this case, the United States Constitution , amendment 14, section 1 states "All persons born or naturalized in the United States and subject to the jurisdiction thereof, are citizens of the United States and of the State wherein they reside. No State shall make or enforce any law which shall abridge the privileges or immunities of citizens of the United States; nor shall any State deprive any person of life, liberty, or property, without due process of law; nor deny to the person within its jurisdiction the equal protection of the laws." So this helps define rights of those who have acceptably become citizens. This offers citizenship and all it entails to the prospective immigrant by going through the naturalization process
    - o In the interest of the country's welfare, certain constraints are applied as overarching to granting citizenship. These include the concept of quota, which is a way of strictly controlling the quantity influx of immigrants so that the system and the country are not overwhelmed with such influx. This also includes the concept of 'vetting, which takes the form of assuring that the immigrant has ability to sustain himself through gainful employment, and also that persons from areas of known threat to this country are carefully examined to assure no threatening intent.

- o There are certain corollaries to aspects of citizenship. And that is why the 'vetting process is critical, to assure that citizenship is clearly understood and that persons can satisfy these guidelines. Whether citizen or not:
    - You do not have a right to wealth, get it legally , but no guarantees
    - You do not have a right to NOT be offended
    - You do not have the right to be free from harm.
    - You have no right to free food, housing, or health care. However, charity can be offered
    - You have no right to physically harm another
    - You have no right to the possessions of others
    - You have no right to a job
    - You have no right to happiness, only to pursue it.
- o Being in this country illegally is ILLEGAL. If laws are changed to create legality, that is the only process that is correct. These laws must be written to insure that transition out of our own laxity does not impose undue burden on the affected.

I feel strongly that coming here illegally violates all the tenets of law and morality. The quota system places persons in a queue in terms of quantity and quality, and circumventing that is inappropriate. Illegality flaunts the nature of boundaries, morality, and lawfulness. As I mentioned, for those to whom the United States has looked away, we are responsible to correct that moral and legal shortfall. But for future situations, there is no excuse for allowing illegality to continue.

We need to engage, we need to look carefully at what it means to serve the best interests of our citizens. I believe that is what "America First" really means.

Figure 4   Kokola, Kaua'i- Gateway

ARTICLE 13   SEX & POWER

I must divert from the discussions centering on "ping-ponging" and politics, and look at a movement that has added to the concept of the "glass ceiling", and with it the consideration that past and current practices and standards need a severe revisit and perhaps a "ping-pong" of their own. It started with private industry, but has spread as well into the political arena. Recently, there has been a very vocal recognition that sexual interactions within our society have included those that are forced, and the current culture had not done anything substantial to challenge that behavior. That basic protest has found its way into the heart and soul of business and government, and brought concern that has added a powerful focus on the qualifications of personnel in any position, and elevated moral compass to at least the same level as experience, past success, awareness, drive, and intelligence. And potentially it is also moving to encompass any form of perceived inequality. It is being used to challenge the qualifications for public office and corporate boardroom. However, what I also see is that in the political arena, dredging up past issues, whether proven or not, has put an onus on the careers of many politicians. If questionable conduct is recent and continuing, then it is rightly an issue. If such conduct can be seen as far-removed past performance, which is no longer being practiced, then further review can be considered appropriate before condemnation occurs.

In terms of morality, power may very well be a considered mechanism for satisfying desires, in that power usage is a method of channeling an asset (for whatever use). The needs of people include food, clothing, shelter, (sex!), and continue down a hierarchical line. As an aside, I just read that paths of emotional reason within the body use our natural-produced dopamine as a channeling device. So what we have is a body that is built to respond to specific stimuli and these stimuli excite the body and reward with satisfaction. The article was actually about the mechanism of opioids and how they grab the channels and eventually create needs within the body for the opioids. I am segueing from this into the fact that sex is a body excitation also and has built-in arousal capability. Sex has many aspects, and right now, one view of sex is that sometimes the expressed desire can be considered offensive, especially if approached in a callous manner. Can't argue that unwanted advances are just that, and pushiness or overtness can surely be offensive. If you get beyond these, into aggressive behavior- watch out.

Sex can be bracketed by its two extremes: pure lust or pure love, and then the breakdown according to how they mix. I'll stop there on the intro, and get right to the point.

I have always felt that "set" and "setting" were part of any conversation. When you apply these, you find that the social mores in existence at one time may be different than at another time, (or even from right now). So when we look back to 30 years ago, we should see a different landscape, perhaps different moral standards, certainly different mental and emotional reactions to any stimuli. Life, liberty, pursuit of happiness- so long as it is between consenting adults and does not harm beyond that consensual line. As we straddle the path of the past to the present, we certainly see growth, or at least change. That is seen both on the part of society's rules and on the part of individuals. Everyone is continuously absorbing input from everywhere- socially, physically, from the government, job-related, financially, aging….. When I wrote 'Moments of Impact", I was looking at what inputs make for change in the individual, all of which can be classified as factors. What I am leading up to now is that alternative paths present themselves for almost all things. Differentiators such as male and female as seen through social eyes are critical to acceptability. So society keeps developing, and rules and regulations, mores and customs, the very fabric of society, are continuously on the move, and perhaps not really "ping-ponging", but actually moving forward. Clearly, tapping into our basic drives is a part of who we are. But I do not condone arbitrary responses to these drives, because we do live within a country that has rules of conduct for its citizens, and these are necessary in order to have a civilized society.

We need to look at power and recognize that power is the driver, sexual conquest is one symptom of exercising it. Bigness is the reality, whether it means you are the boss, or you have wealth, or some other "attribute"- really it relates to some of your property and how you use it. Recognizing that food and sex provide two of the basic pleasures of life, we may have opposing perspectives on interactions in this arena. When a person can use something to advantage, is that acceptable? Is it a thing that our society has expected can be done? By the way, there are two sides to each element, and each of us having assets of interest has the privilege of utilizing these to benefit ourselves. I am not necessarily applying it to specific situations, just looking at the mores of our society. In consideration of general mores is the idea of property and respect, both of which must be applied to each societal aspect in order to truly assure the good "ole" American Dream of freedom to pursue your rights to life, liberty, and the pursuit of happiness (so long as it does not impose on another). Which trumps which? That is the question. It is clear to me that if your property is being violated, *that* trumps all other aspects, because protection and respect of and for property is key to societal living.

I need some help here. There are two perspectives to examine. If one party <u>approaches</u> and states desire, and the other party agrees; or as the other party is <u>approached</u> and then consents, with or without benefits, isn't this mutually "consensual"? Notice that I said "party", no gender mentioned. Only if it is done without <u>consent</u> does it transfer from a state of <u>consensual</u> agreement between two <u>consenting</u> adults into a state of forced action on the property of another. Of course there are secondary actions and situations, such as the use of foul language, inadvertent touching without consent, lewdness placed in plain sight, etc..... and these things are specific violations of social convention. But they are somewhat different than forcible action on a party without their consent.
And so, when it comes to power and sex, it can be a two-way street between two parties, and the key is mutual consent. That is the only way it can work without moral or social shortfall. "I can't take it anymore" is acceptable, but going back and recognizing other times, other standards, other conditions that have been affected by "remoteness dilution" (time and memory), must be a part of the package in that what is now considered wrong may have previously

been considered only as undesirable, or even tacitly condoned (hate to say it, but sometimes an asset is used as a tool to further ambition).

The reason this article is presented is because of dredging up of incidents from the long ago past, things of indiscretion whose realities suffer from memory of the event, perspective at the time, and perhaps a non-recognition that our youthful past is a phase we often outgrow. This, in contrast to continuing behavior that clearly represents a recent or current mind-set.

CONCLUSIONS: SO WHERE ARE WE GOING?

I have said a lot. I know I have pontificated somewhat. And I put out a rather simple study effort in the appendix, one that really needs so much more substantiation, but yet does offer insights through trend. Mainly however, my thrust has been about mind-set, and the fact that politics has corrupted the thinking powers of the elected. Every single one of these august representatives of the people, duly elected or selected, needs to embed within their thinking and moral processes the thoughts that the intent is protection of life, liberty, and pursuit of happiness of the citizenry they represent. And rather than politics, the mind-set should be diplomacy, because politics is about power, while diplomacy is about getting things done.

Human Nature is something that has evolved over the development of human-kind, and our intellect has not gained control over all aspects of it. In fact, our roots as animals and our developed human nature still shine in most of the things we do, and why we do them. So the idea of "ping-pong", the idea of back and forth, the idea of continual loops, is one we have deeply ingrained in our psyche. And it shows, because what I have written so far, although slanted by my own predilections, still tells a tale and shows how far we are from completing the journey. Maybe when we recognize that life is the journey, and there really is no final goal to achieve, then we will step back and begin the recognition that it is most important to *enjoy*, not to *struggle*. So onward and upward, towards aspirations which in fact merely draw us along the path- this is truly our goal.

And speaking of human nature, property is a key. It represents what is innate within us, the way we have translated our capabilities into livable commodity. We must be proud of what we are, what we offer, what we do, and no one should take these things away from us. Proud does not mean flaunt, it means satisfaction, and it means a full life.
This ends the formal aspect of this missive, I hope it had something to offer the reader, and has piqued curiosity, intellect, and emotion sufficiently to warrant further thought. I really do hope so, because I

truly believe that our political system has run amok, and that we are being steered by rudders that have little regard for what this country's basic pillars of foundation offer. In a free-enterprise democracy, we must allow what I call the "ping-pong" effect, but only in order to generate the smoothing towards forward flow as we try to firm up our path and direction for a healthy, hardy, happy future.

Joe

ADDENDUM 1   PROGRAM STUDY: HEALTH CARE

(This section relates to article 5 of the text.)

MISSION STATEMENT: Health is a critical parameter in support of life, liberty, and the pursuit of happiness. Health is your own- it is considered as specific to each individual. If you choose to ruin your health by exposing yourself to health-danger by your choice of work, life-style, living conditions... that is up to you the individual. On the other hand, normal living will expose each of us to the normal environment that places health-risk into the equation through accidents, communicable disease, birth defect, age. *IT IS NECESSARY TO ESTABLISH IF THERE IS A NEED TO INVOLVE THE GOVERNMENT IN THIS PROCESS, TO WHAT DEGREE IF SO, AND* **TO DEFINE A PROGRAM THAT CAN SATISFY BASIC REQUIREMENTS FOR ASSURING THAT THE CITIZENRY CAN ESTABLISH AND THEN HAVE APPROPRIATE AVAILABILITY OF COVERAGE THROUGH EITHER HEALTH INSURANCE OR HEALTH CARE.**

OBJECTIVE: To develop and select choices for methods of supporting a health care system that will satisfy the needs of all citizens to obtain their own defined health care requirements.

VALUES: We live in a free-enterprise democracy, one that offers that each of us can exchange our work effort for remuneration and thence translate that into obtaining the commodities desired for our lives. Across the spectrum of the work environment there is a large range of salaries for work performed, and therefore a major distribution difference of monetary availability for life's necessities. **EACH PERSON SHOULD HAVE THE ABILITY TO PROTECT HIS LIFE, LIBERTY, AND PURSUIT OF HAPPINESS.**

PREMISES:

- Each citizen is to establish his/her own translation of capability for work into a method for obtaining sufficiency for living.
- If unsatisfied with results, then improve your own capability to increase your livelihood. Through either personal effort to encompass (self-) education, or through either government or private funding, availability for (self-) education to increase earning capability exists. Use it.
- Government's role in any (health) system is to allow free market forces to operate and to prevent monopoly from instituting strangleholds on (in this instance) either medical care or medical supplies.
- Any welfare system offered through government support is limited to
    - Helping place work-capable persons into the job market
    - Offering interim and time-limited support until self-sufficiency is obtained
    - Support for those who cannot work, but only as minimally required
    - Charitable organizations also exist to assist the "no-work-capability" poverty level persons.

ACTIONS: This study is undertaken to define a health care system for the country that satisfies the expectations of the rules above by using the parameters of COST, PERFORMANCE, SCHEDULE, SUPPORTABILITY, and RISK in a trade study (Matrix of Alternatives) that shows the nature of the various choices and their attributes and shortfalls. *Risk in this case is associated with the completeness of integrating the specific alternative, and the assurance that it will meet all the criteria defined. It is programmatic risk, and must include as far as possible, elements that address technical risk. If they cannot be quantified, this becomes programmatic risk. Performance is associated with both the specific system as defined, and its ability to meet the criteria for health care availability.*

SELECTION CRITERIA:　　　At the completion of the Matrix of Alternatives, and the inclusion of the parameters defining each selection, "MEASURES OF MERIT" (MOM) will be assigned to allow comparison of the alternatives and the selection of the recommended solution. Part of the MOM will be at least a discussion of the life cycle or cost benefit perspective, which would be the arithmetic summation of the up-front-cost plus the long-term supportability cost.   Inherent will be the impact of the risk assessment. As well, since this subject involves the well-being and lives of the recipients, special factors within the risk assessment must recognize where shortfalls exist, and how to deal with them. <u>I believe that cost to the general taxpayer for each alternative would probably be the closest to a total MOM, because that is where the overall effectiveness of the system is really measured, given that minimum performance objectives are met.</u> Not looking to offer more than minimum unless an individual is willing to pony up him- or herself.

ALTERNATIVE CONFIGURATIONS FOR THIS STUDY:
So let's define some of the alternative choices for configurations that will be used to satisfy the "Health Program's" parameters, remembering that in all cases, government's function should be only to prevent capitalistic monopoly which could impair the implementation of the letter and availability of a system, and to protect the citizen rights to life, liberty, and the pursuit of happiness as it applies to this study. And again, to provide choice to the citizen, the ability to determine how to meet his/her own health needs. This is **my** ground rule, maybe not acceptable to all, but a premise of this study. The alternatives deliberately range from no programs to full and absolute coverage, to allow the fall-out of the effort to include extremes.

ALTERNATIVE 1- <u>A Free Enterprise Capitalistic Marketplace without any insurance.</u> Such a system is based on the ability of the individual to reach his own agreement with each aspect of the medical community, the prescription community, and the care community that suitable payment for services rendered will be guaranteed. Cost of these services and time for payment would be individually negotiated between the parties. This is the way things were before health insurance. It is acknowledged that in this system, people are responsible to themselves to assure life-protective care availability.

ALTERNATIVE 2- <u>A Free Enterprise Marketplace with ranges of available health insurance and choice of your own individual healthcare providers.</u> This system would consider that Health Insurance is the method providing the costs for defined services required. This insurance would range in choice from catastrophic minimums to full support, and would be priced according to free market principles of supply and demand. Each insured individual would have choice of medical service providers, and would be insured only for the specified amounts of the policy, costs above to be borne by the insured, costs below to be reimbursed or pre-paid at specified amounts.

ALTERNATIVE 3- <u>A Free Market of Selectable Insurance Plans inclusive of Healthcare providers.</u> This system (PPO or HMO) takes advantage of the cost synergies that result from combining functions to provide a full market capability. Various insurers would have established relationships with various providers.

ALTERNATIVE 4- <u>Government Run Health Market.</u> This is a single payer system, run in a non-competitive market, where all services are defined and priced by the single payer. The cost of the program would come through taxation and fees and would be set by the government. The scope of the medical support within the program would be set by the government. This is not merely an insurance umbrella for care, it is a provider of care as well. This definition of alternative is made to represent the extreme antithesis of any of the other building block configurations. This way, a stark comparison will be available for developing the MOMs. That is why it is discussed up front and immediately in the following paragraph.

It does however, offer "challenges".
- Is it morally appropriate to TAKE from one and give to another without their consent? This through either tax or fee (or perhaps called plunder) and placed in the government pot.
- On the other hand, is it a moral shortfall not to provide care to someone else?
- What is the definition of "appropriate" in terms of health care?

- What are the salaries of the health workers-who sets them, who defines them, who selects the workers in this essentially non-competitive environment?
- Who selects the committee members who will make the rules, interpret the rules, enforce the rules?
- What is the cost basis for the services? In a non-competitive environment, which need not operate at a profit, and which receives its budget based on need, there is essentially an unlimited source of funding.
- Will there be sufficient skilled worker personnel to satisfy the need with salaries and working conditions defined by a monopoly, and will the need be defined by any of the parameters of competition, such as performance, wait times, quality of service, availability of service?
- Will there be a hierarchy of service offerings, going from catastrophic minimums to a "platinum" totality? If so, how to quantify and qualify?
- Will there be caps placed on insurance payouts?

COSTS OF EACH ALTERNATIVE:

For this study, this does not include the non-recurring development and acquisition costs to establish the program. *It does include the recurring operating costs for running the program, but not any further non-recurring costs to maintain the program.* This will be translated back into its basic cost to each individual, and to the overall system.   I feel that the costing premises below are completely scalable based on the magnitude of the assumptions.

Costing Premises- (recognizing that these are arbitrarily established here simply to provide a baseline) .   For all of the various alternatives, extending from 40 years or changing the nuclear family size to anything greater will accentuate any differences, but these differences are already shown based on this premise.

- Family of 4, term span per family considered to be 40 years of coverage.

- o The reasons for this premise is that now the specific amounts per person that are assumed can be averaged over 4 people, and the occurrence of events can be averaged over 40 years. Thus, individual events can be distributed amongst 4 people and 40 years to help define a more suitable average
- Two major hospitalizations/lifetime for each person, at $100,000/occurrence
- Two doctor's visits for each person/year, at $300/visit
- Pharmaceutical costs at $400/year/person
- If purchasing insurance only, set the above as the maximum expense for a minimum cost policy offering, and therefore an out-of-pocket **maximum** expected cost/ person for 40 years would be $200,000+$24,000+$16000= $240,000/person. See probability curves at the end of this cost section to support the cost of insurance- this is based on the following distribution curve of probabilities: 25% of policy holders get pay-out at a cost of under $30,000, 50% under $60,000, 75% under $100,000, and 100% under the $240,000. Such a distribution would cost the insurance companies an outlay of roughly $80,000/person over 40 years. Allowing an infrastructure cost of 25% and a profit margin of 25%, the **average** cost of the policy over the 40 years would be 1.5 X $80,000=$120,000 or $3000/year/person. The terms of payoff against a health care event would be part of the policy and would be commensurate with the distribution premised.
- Costs are calculated as "now-costs", without the rigor of considering inflation, therefore 40 year totals and averages would actually be even higher in "then-year" dollars, by a significant amount. For the purposes of comparison, simply look at the ratio of costs for each alternative.
- Let me start by defining the individual cost above as the baseline. It recognizes that this would be the average cost to the average citizen, obtained by dividing the total cost by the number of citizens, wherein the many at low cost and the few at high cost are all acknowledged in producing what could be defined as the universal citizens average cost for lifetime healthcare.

ALTERNATIVE 1 - "No insurance"
Here is an option that essentially goes back to the early years of our country, a time when there was direct interaction between patient and doctor, apothecary, hospital, if such existed. Because it is based on each individual paying his own way, there is an obvious sliding care scale, wherein the more you can afford, the more you can get. It therefore stratifies health care significantly, and for those without monetary reserves, requires either going without, charity, getting a loan, or bartering for future payment. It also can offer preventative care, but recognize that for certain income levels, this will not be a selected choice.
There will be no over-riding network of coordination or management with respect to an individual. All services are contracted by the individual.
Using the above premises, a family of four would reach a spending profile of no more than $960,000 over 40 years. This is a *maximum* cost. This would be a cost of $6,0000/year/ family member. Based on the profile and logic presented in the costing premises, the *average* cost would be $3000/year/family member.

ALTERNATIVE 2   - "Free Selective Choice"
You can pick your doctor, hospital, pharmacy, and you also separately pick your insurance provider and the scope of your health insurance plan. This is the first iteration into the world of health insurance. It looks ahead with an eye towards recognizing that health care costs can be expensive, and that purchasing future protection for unknown circumstances requires careful consideration. (Amazing, it's like auto insurance also used to be). It is akin to the way things were handled before government subsidies entered the equation. Obviously there are many premises and ground rules required in order to implement a properly structured set of mechanisms. In the free marketplace concept competition would offer the both the highest and lowest bang for the buck among the alternatives.   It must be premised that such a condition can be made to exist. For example, that there are sufficient medical personnel in the general medical pool to satisfy needs and requirements.   Also that there are sufficient sources of medication and care available, so that excess pricing will fail and that marginal producers will leave the market place. If these things happen, then a real system of health care can be initiated, including degrees of preventative medicine.
This will give the buyer choices for extent of care and cost and caps of care.

In the insurance industry, pricing is based on probability and actuarial analysis. So looking at the premises, and the profile established as the baseline, and actuarial data for distribution of health requirements (see curves below), the health billing to a family of four over a 40 year period would be covered up to $960,000. The average family cost would be $240,000, or $1500/year/family member.

ALTERNATIVE 3 -"The PPO"
As industry recognizes competition, there is always a drive and incentive to do one better. In this case, strategic alliances are premised to be formed to offer vertical and horizontal integration by entities that would offer complete health insurance **and** health care. The benefit of this model is that it becomes optimized for least cost and best service. It allows the consumer to make his own decision as to which plan and which supplier makes the most sense, and it lets the consumer know by looking at the market place, whether one PPO offers more than another. It also takes away the worry of picking the best for the job, because each package represents itself through its reputation, and that would be a well-known item in the marketplace. Because each PPO advertises itself and its attributes, it behooves each one to select the best in all services and to offer at the lowest price for these services. With maximum payout coverage recognizing that the amount would now offer perhaps 30% more than the original calculation and with the max insured amount remaining the same, the actual cost for the identical coverage would drop proportionately by 30% to $1050/year/family member.

ALTERNATIVE 4 -"Single Payer Government Health Care"
Competition does not exist in this model, only the authority to do "the job". In this alternative, control is centered within the narrowly defined market of the single offering entity. The cost for running this program, and the cost of providing its benefits, lies in the taxation and fee realm, which means (like it or not) <u>you</u> will pay and typically, taxes would rise to meet the need. The scope, depth, and breadth of the program will be defined by the government and its appointees to the various committees set up to run the program. Overseeing agencies that monitor the policies and procedures will be appointed by the government. The program relies on the moral judgements and the professional inputs of personnel as assigned by the government

agencies; less on the economics of reality. As with so many government programs (among them social security, welfare, unemployment, the government budget, national debt), since the till is always full through further taxation or poor fiscal policy such as continued and increasing debt, this program is boundless in its future abilities. The only possible control will be the voices of the citizenry, and it will be a polarized set of cries, on the one hand for more benefits, on the other the plea for less taxation.

In reviewing this cost, the model needs to incorporate a higher level of bureaucracy, a lower level of value (due to less competition), and perhaps more than that, a shift in the probability curve to reflect that a higher percentage of the population will now be enrolled and will make use of available services because the price is a shared value adjusted by a taxation schedule that recognizes a sliding tax scale. So several assumptions will be modified to perform this portion of the analysis. There is a revised distribution of usage, and then a look at average costs per use per person rather than the actual tax schedule of highest income pays most. Again, see curves below.

Revised Distribution of Usage: distribution curve of probabilities: 25% of policy holders at a payout cost of under $50,000, 50% under $100,000, 75% under $160,000, and 100% under the $240,000. Such a distribution would incur a cost of roughly $110,000 over 40 years or $2700/year/person. There is no government "profit", but there will be expenses for personnel to run the enterprise, above and beyond the healthcare professionals, as well as normal overhead expenses, and these will at least equal the costs of running businesses. Therefore, a 50% tab will be placed on the direct costs, similar to what would be the case for private industry. This would increase the average cost to $4000/year/person. To look at a sliding taxation scale for this option, the premise is that 25% do not pay into a health insurance tax (they are subsidized), 50% pay the average of $4000/year/person, 16% pay $6000, and 9% pay $12,000/year/person.

Next needs to be a distribution of taxation that would support the premise that government control will in fact offer "Affordable Health Care" to all, regardless of performance level.

The Distribution of usage assigned to Option 2 approximates the distribution of wealth as well, since in option 1 each person pays his own way, and must figure how to afford that. When then considering cost versus taxation, the average recipient would have a shortfall of ($4000-$1500) =$2500/year/person. This amount would be obtained from a sliding tax scale that would take more from those who had and essentially support those in the lower brackets (see charts below, based on now-dollars).

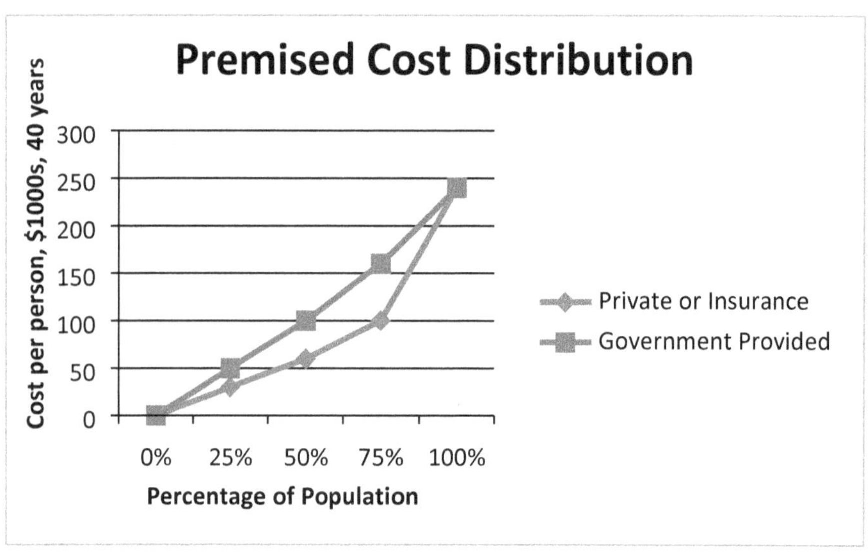

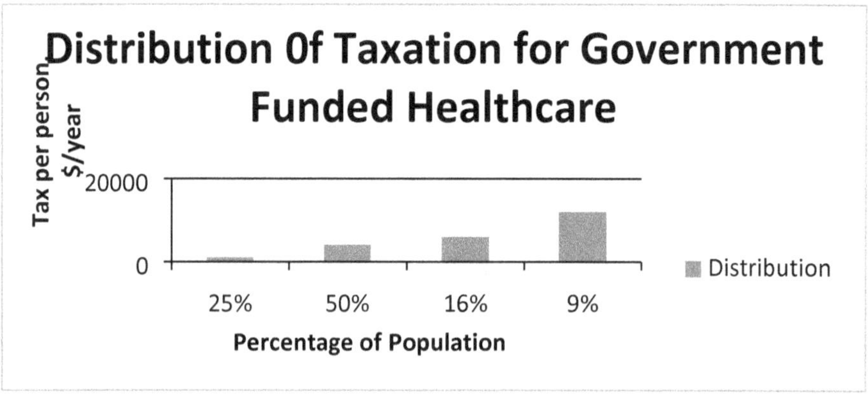

PERFORMANCE OF EACH ALTERNATIVE

ALTERNATIVE 1- "No Insurance"
In a system that is strictly free enterprise with private companies offering their medical services to those who are willing to contract with them, there will be a significant range of treatments, equipment, procedures. Performance will be based on ability to pay, and selection of the provider by each individual will have to be a balance between reputation and affordability. This will be a free market decision, and thence competitive, plus there will be many "small business" choices, ie.. the country doctor, the local pharmacy. Additionally, use of the profession will be tied more to need than desire. Even catastrophic care will become choice for the patient (home vs facility). Loans may be the method of choice for payments. One thing this alternative really requires is thoughtfulness about the future and per the premises of the study, the desire of each person to improve their work condition to improve their available savings.

ALTERNATIVE 2- "Free (Selective) Choice"
Because the concept of insurance has entered the marketplace, this choice is the first step towards assuring necessary care. It consists of two selection aspects for the insured; an insurance vehicle selection consisting of company and scope, and the personnel selection of the medical team of doctors, medication suppliers, and facilities. To the extent that the insured does due diligence, this alternative is a significant step above the "no insurance option", in that careful consideration of insurance type will assure the kind of coverage that is desired at a cost that is affordable for the insured, with outlay capped by the insurance company policy. The medical side requires that the patient look at reputation and do a careful study to get the best service.

ALTERNATIVE 3- "The PPO"
This is the epitome of the free market choices, because examination of each group's offering includes reputations of insurer and its service providers, scope of coverage, cost of coverage. Based on the premise that the oversight that the government provides will assure that monopoly will not occur; then each competitive PPO must offer the best packages for each cost and scope increment. By combining all services under one banner, the

services will either fall short professionally and cause the marginal PPO to falter or regroup, or the group will rise within the market choices.

ALTERNATIVE 4- "Single Payer Government Healthcare"
The concept has merit if the goals and the implementation are correct. However, the idea that cost need be controlled has two prongs, and neither necessarily for the betterment of service.   Without competition, the standard of excellence has no criteria. Additionally, the cost of service has no comparative base. Offering packages of coverage is not under control, because the lack of requirement for type of service, time for service, staffing, content of offerings, agreement on cost and coverage, all fall under the umbrella of non-competition. Setting up panels of experts to determine scope of each category of coverage, cost of such coverage, eligibility for either coverage or re-imbursement, rules governing rapidity of service, etc......are all under the auspices of a single entity- the government.

SCHEDULE OF IMPLEMENTATION

Each alternative has certain basics that are common to all. These start with coverage- there already are many qualified professional personnel and facilities to perform necessary functions. Whether there are adequate resources will be dependent on free market conditions, even in the case of "Single Payer Government HealthCare".   This is where the issue of resource availability comes into play. However, it seems that schedule can be acceptable in terms of up to 8 years or so to implement because there are already systems in place, and this study is to recommend a replacement which can come on line in a traditional incremental manner. Therefore, schedule will be treated more as a comparative length of time between alternatives, not as a criterion for selection.

ALTERNATIVE 1- "No Insurance"
At this point in the definition of the United States of America, a "no health insurance option" does exist, but infrastructure within the country is expecting that insurance is and will continue to be available. Return to a "no

insurance option" would require the establishment of a withdrawal methodology that leaves people with equivalent optional capability to what insurance had offered. This could be savings accounts, or loan programs, or charitable ventures. Dismantling and establishing is premised at 5 years.

ALTERNATIVE 2- "Free Selective Choice"
This is essentially where we are today, except that "ACA" has been injected into the marketplace. ACA would be either eliminated or restructured dropping out certain requirements, but in either case there would be more focus on the free market offering more than is available today. This would mean more choice in both insurance plan scope and in costs of any form of care. Modifying what is available today could be done within 3 years.

ALTERNATIVE 3- "PPO"
PPO's are a part of today's market place, but in this instance the concept differentiation from alternative 2 is that conglomerates, vertically and horizontally integrated, would offer full option capability. It would take 4 years to generate the integration onto full PPO.

ALTERNATIVE 4- "Single Payer Government Healthcare"
This would be a massive blending of all medical abilities into one large infrastructure that would provide full care, would manage the rules and regulations, the availability, all policies and procedures. It is estimated that 8 years would be necessary to set up a single payer system that could handle all health care.

SUPPORTABILITY
This is the subject of follow-on service after the alternative has been selected. It includes support costs to run the program, both hardware and operating expenses including salaries of personnel, costs of facilities, etc... This section defines the actual cost of operation.

ALTERNATIVE 1- "No Insurance"
This alternative does not cost the taxpayer any money aside from caring for him/herself and family as and when required . It does place those at low income level at a disadvantage in that they either have their own health-savings, divert their own funds from other costs, or take out loans to satisfy up-front medical costs. I am not talking about those who cannot in any way work to support themselves, because those people will obtain funding through a charitable or actual no-work/poverty supplement. Rules will assure that absolute minimums are provided.

ALTERNATIVE 2- "Free Selective Choice"
This alternative does not cost the taxpayer any money, as discussed above. What it does however, is offer those on lower pay scales the option for catastrophic care or any level above that which is considered minimally affordable. It offers a look at the future. Considering the above, any charitable or supplemental funding would be even less than above, because it is through an insurance pool.

ALTERNATIVE 3- "PPO"
This alternative also does not cost the taxpayer any money, as discussed in alternates 1 and 2. Because by definition, the PPO is even less expensive than the "Free Selective Choice" in that vertical and horizontal integration within the PPO has reduced its costs, this alternative is less expensive than alt 1 or 2.

ALTERNATIVE 4- "Single Payer Government Healthcare"
Here is the major diversion of thinking from the chain-linked alternatives above. This is a methodology that levels the playing field through taxation or fee on everyone, presumably proportional to wealth, and distributing this funding (less salaries and cost of government business) to everyone, proportional to need. It has the merit of **providing** care to any and all, and could be structured in benefit tiers. It does however, offer "challenges", as discussed in the definition of alternatives.
- Is it morally appropriate to TAKE from one and give to another without their consent?
- Is it morally appropriate not to provide care to someone else?

- What is "appropriate" ?
- Who controls worker work definition?
- Who selects the rule-makers?
- What is the cost basis for the services?
- Will there be sufficient skilled worker personnel to satisfy the need.
- Will there be a hierarchy of service offerings?

RISK

ALTERNATIVE 1- "No Insurance"
This selection does not produce risk per say. What it does is note that without insurance, health care becomes potentially unaffordable for those who cannot obtain necessary funding needs. This is not a programmatic risk, because under this definition, each individual is responsible for himself and family and knowing that, needs to identify methods of handling health issues. BUT, it is no assurance of receiving care, and so RISK here means access to care, which really means that people need to work hard to assure financial capability to get certain care. Charity offers one form of care payment, and welfare for the totally unemployable represents another.

ALTERNATIVE 2- "Free Selective Choice"
The cost of various alternative health plans, ranging from no insurance to high level, requires that alternatives at the lowest end must be affordable. Choice of having insurance versus giving up some other element of living is one that must always be made by the individual. This alternative offers that insurance is available, but that each insured person must select their own care parameters and personnel. It puts care providers on notice that each and every one of them is in a strongly competitive marketplace and must therefore offer the strongest possible reputation for them to be selected by the patient. Risk exists not to the programmatics, but as a function of the healthcare entities selected by the patient.

ALTERNATIVE 3- "PPO"
So long as the concept of a competitive marketplace is protected, horizontal and vertical integration into PPO's is a positive one. The onus of picking individual aspects of health care is no longer on the patient, but on the PPO. There is no programmatic risk. There is no risk to recipients.

ALTERNATIVE 4-   "Single Payer Government Healthcare"
The competitive market no longer exists in this option. The risk is to the potential runaway nature of the only existing entity. It looms large, because care is in the hands of a monopoly and costs are not constrained, however, everyone would get SOME care, although not assured of timeliness or completeness.

MEASURES OF MERIT

Comparison is always a potentially biased methodology. In this particular case, weighing all the parameters against the definitions and requirements of the study is especially difficult because although all choices offer the ability to obtain care, degrees of performance may not completely offer satisfaction to all. However, this will be pointed out as part of the decision matrix below.

Ratings will be assigned based on "A" being highest or best, and "D" being lowest or worst.

The discussions leading to these ratings were presented above in each of the various sections.

HEALTH INSURANCE/CARE TRADE STUDY MATRIX

(family of 4, averaged over 40 years, see premises)

Notes: 1- See discussions above, of Alt 4 costs

ALTERNATIVE/ PARAMETER	1-NO INSUR- ANCE	2-INS CHOICE	3-PPO	4-GOVT RUN	COMMENT
COST TO RECIPIENT- $/year/family member (in terms of direct cost or taxation)	$240,000/ 40= $6000 max. $3000 avg.	$1500	$1050	Sliding scale[1]: $0.0 min $4000 avg $12000 max	[1] For Alt 4, depend- ent on tax bracket, some families pay $0, while some Pay $6000-$12000
40 year cost for family of 4	$480,000 avg $960,000 max	$240,000 avg	$168,000 avg	AVG $640,000 min=$0.0[1], max=$1,920 ,000	[1] For Alt 4, min is based on full subsidiza- tion
COST RATIOS	1.0	0.5	0.35	1.33	
PERFORMANCE (in terms of care)	D	B	A	C	Alt 1 ignores insurance, puts some persons in financial jeopardy
SCHEDULE (to implementation)	5 years to withdra w from today's mix	3 years to integrate	4 years to integrate	8 years to consolidate and set up controls	Any of the schedules is acceptable
SUPPORT- ABILITY	A	A	A	D	Alt 4 is fraught with unknown future cost to support
RISK	C	B	A	D	Alt 4- cost with marginal perform- ance per lack of competition
MOM (Measure of Merit)	C	B	A	D	

STUDY CONCLUSIONS AND DISCUSSION:

As you can see in the matrix and the establishment of the ratings, there can be lots of room for disagreement. Alternative 1 (no insurance), and alternative 4 (government run) are the two extremes and are most sensitive to the premises established to generate the matrix. The logic for these two is the basis of all the premises. Without insurance, clearly families are on their own, must make extreme choices as to how to spend, borrow, or save their money, and consider the limitations they will undergo when looking at health care requirements during time of injury or ill health. With government single payer healthcare, care limitations such as cost, actual procedures, wait times for and at appointments, staffing and salaries, rules for coverage, redress, etc... are some of the potential issues. Looking at government sponsored health care in other countries, there is no question that competitive choices offer better performance conditions in all aspects except cost to those who cannot afford coverage, **AND this alternative is one where SUBSIDY on the sliding scale represents the premise that health care is a RIGHT, rather than a CHOICE.**

But it all comes down to the fact that Alternative 3, the PPO, is the least expensive and offers the most in health care availability and performance. And for both alternatives 2 and 3, it is necessary to premise that those who absolutely cannot work will be provided some form of subsidy for care, and that this will establish the absolute minimum plan to be offered by the PPO's. Part of that cost will be spread into a specific form of average cost of care. Such things as pre-conditions will be accepted, and the costs for such extreme care will also be part of this average, but there will be a major incentive for the insurance companies to subsidize research to eliminate the occurrence of such medical pre-conditions, thereby reducing the need for extreme care.

Study Summary

In all, because single-payer (Alt 4) has so many unknowns that all tend to
raise cost and lower performance, it is necessary to consider that the PPO
(Alt 3) offers the best from a programmatic perspective- the best
performance, the least cost, the least risk, and by the way, is commensurate
with the concept of a free economy.

REFERENCES

1. Rand, Ayn <u>Capitalism</u>, 1967
2. Galambos, Andrew J., <u>Sic Itar Ad Astra</u>, vol. 1, 1999
3. Harriman, David (editor), <u>Journals of Ayn Rand</u>, 1999
4. Hazlitt, Henry, <u>Economics in One Easy Lesson</u>, 1979
5. Roosevelt, Teddy, <u>Letter of January, 1919</u>, archived in Manuscript Division of Library of Congress

Got any comments to this entire document? Have I posed any interesting situations? Note them and modify your own perception of what I have written by what you now believe. I would gladly receive these comments for discussion.

Joe

baluku1@hotmail.com

COMMENTS

<u>Page, Section</u>　　　　　　　　**<u>What I, the reader, believe</u>**

JUST A BIT OF BIO:

Joe Goldstein was born in 1938 in New York City, and currently resides in Los Angeles, California with his wife Donna. He worked in aerospace for 42 years, with specialties in analysis, system engineering, and project management. Amongst his passions is sensitivity to the sanctity of personal property, and a strong desire to understand man's drives for fulfillment in this wonderful life we all live.

His web-site and catalogue of books can be seen by pasting this link into your header.
https://www.josephkgoldstein.com
 or "google"   Joseph K Goldstein and see what's available

(Look for the "America, Evolving Personality" description)